WJEC Vocational Award

Hospitality and Catering
Level 1/2

Study & Revision Guide

Anita Tull

Illuminate
Publishing

Published in 2020 by Illuminate Publishing Ltd,
P.O. Box 1160, Cheltenham, Gloucestershire GL50 9RW

Orders: Please visit www.illuminatepublishing.com
or email sales@illuminatepublishing.com

British Library Cataloguing in Publication Data

A catalogue record for this book is available from the British Library

ISBN 978-1-912820-17-7

Printed in the UK by Cambrian Printers, Aberystwyth

02.20

The publisher's policy is to use papers that are natural, renewable
and recyclable products made from wood grown in sustainable
forests. The logging and manufacturing processes are expected to
conform to the environmental regulations of the country of origin.

Publisher: Claire Hart

Editor: Geoff Tuttle

Design and layout: Nigel Harriss

Cover image: Shutterstock.com / goodluz

Dedication

With many thanks to Alison Palmer for her help with reviewing this
book at manuscript and proof stages.

Acknowledgements

Reproduced with kind permission of Nisbets Plc:

p31 chopping boards; p32 chopping boards and knives; p33 catering kitchen
materials; p52 slip-on shoes, chain mail glove, freezer gloves; p56 anti-
fatigue mat; p60 anti-fatigue mat, trolley; p61 slicer with safety guard, deep
fat frying machine, knife wallet; p152 bottles, mousse ring, plating wedge,
tweezers; p153 chip scoop

p59 Allergen menu reproduced with the kind permission of Prezzo

p60 sit-stand stool reproduced with the kind permission of LOTZ Lagertechnik
GmbH, Germany

p110–111 graphs contain public sector information licensed under the Open
Government Licence v3.0.

CONTENTS

You will find suggested answers to Knowledge check, Practice questions and Stretch and challenge questions from the book, online: www.illuminatepublishing.com/srghosp&cateranswers

Introduction

This study and revision guide has been written to help you get ready for the online e-assessment in Unit 1 (this can also be taken as a written examination) and the controlled assessment task that you will do for Unit 2 in the WJEC Vocational Award in Hospitality and Catering Level 1/2 qualification.

Chapter 14 in the student textbook gives you more information about the types of questions you may be asked in the Unit 1 e-assessment and Chapter 28 gives more details about the Unit 2 controlled assessment task.

How to use this study and revision guide

Unit 1: The Hospitality and Catering industry

How much of the qualification is this worth?	40%

Unit 1 covers the following topics:

- All the different parts of the Hospitality and Catering (H&C) industry
- Different types of hospitality and catering establishments and job roles
- Different types of hospitality and catering provision for particular situations
- Front of house and kitchen operations
- The needs and requirements of customers
- What makes hospitality and catering businesses successful
- Issues related to nutrition and food safety.

What do you have to do?

Answer questions on a variety of topics either online on a computer, or as a written examination.

Unit 2: Hospitality and Catering in Action

How much of the qualification is this worth?	60%

Unit 2 asks you to apply what you have learned by: planning, preparing, cooking and serving a variety of healthy, tasty and appetising dishes that are suitable for different situations and customer needs and requirements, in a safe and hygienic way.

What do you have to do?

Apply what you have learned to a Learner Assignment Brief, which will give you a scenario that you have to answer. You will write an account of what you have done and take a practical cooking assessment to show your skills.

Good luck on your course. We hope that you will enjoy learning about Hospitality and Catering, and will develop your skills and confidence as you progress through the course and possibly onto further training and a career in this industry.

Features to help you

Throughout the book, there are a number of features to help you to study and progress through the course, which are shown below:

Activity

A range of activities are given throughout the book. They are designed to help you learn a topic more thoroughly and practise answering questions.

Key terms

These give you the definitions of the key terminology (words) in each of the topics that you need to know and use.

Refers to the relevant pages from the student book so you can refer back for more detail if you want to.

Knowledge check – can you remember....?

These are end-of-topic questions that are designed to help you remember key points when you are revising for the Unit 1 assessment.

E-assessment practice questions

These are end-of-topic questions, written in different styles and with a range of command words. They are designed to give you the chance to practise and improve the way you answer questions.

Scenario

These are activities that use realistic situations/proposals/problems that occur in hospitality and catering. You are asked to consider and make suggestions as to how these situations would be dealt with and/or suggest a suitable option for hospitality and catering provision, and/or suggest solutions to the problems presented.

Stretch and challenge questions

These are activities/questions in which you will need to find out more about a topic and practise being able to answer questions at a higher level, showing your detailed knowledge and understanding.

Photographs and drawings: there are many of these throughout the book. They are included to help you further understand and visualise a topic.

The Hospitality and Catering industry

What do you need to know? (AC1.1)

- How the H&C industry is structured
- The jobs and services it provides
- How it is rated for different sets of standards

Chapter 1

Book link
pp8–21

LO1 Understand the environment in which hospitality and catering providers operate

Key learning

The H&C industry is one of the biggest employers in the UK. It uses many outside agencies, businesses and people to supply it with everything it needs.

Hospitality means providing people with a place to stay (accommodation), meals, drinks and entertainment in a variety of places.

Catering means providing people with a food and drink service in a variety of places.

Caterers supply businesses and places with food that is made in a central kitchen/factory, then delivered to order.

Key terms you should try to include in your answers

Caterers – supply businesses and places (establishments) with food made in a central kitchen/factory, then delivered to order

Catering – providing people with food and drink in a variety of places

Hospitality – providing people with accommodation, meals, drinks and entertainment in a variety of places

---

The structure of the Hospitality and Catering industry

Hospitality
Somewhere to stay (accommodation), food, drinks and entertainment

+

Catering
Food and drinks

Where?
Hotels, guest houses, bed and breakfast, inns, pubs, farmhouses, holiday camps and parks, family cabins, luxury camping (glamping), cruise ships, long-distance trains, airlines, motorway services, youth hostels

Suppliers provide:
Agency staff / employees (temporary and permanent)
Cleaning materials
Drinks
Equipment
Flower arrangements
Food
Furniture
Laundering services (washing and drying clothes and bed sheets, etc.)
Tableware – knives, forks, spoons, glasses, plates, etc.
Uniforms
Waste disposal
etc.

Where?
Restaurants, bistros, dining rooms, canteens, cafes, tearooms, coffee shops, takeaway and fast food outlets, pubs, bars, clubs, casinos, street food, pop-up restaurants, mobile/ roadside food vans, motorway services, visitor and tourist attractions (theme parks, museums, zoos, etc.), sport stadiums, concert/gig venues, hospitals, schools, prisons, care homes, people's homes (parties, funerals, etc.)

Types of food service systems

Book link
pp9–10

What do you need to know?

- How food is served to people in different ways (food service systems) in different places (establishments)

Counter service

- Customers choose food from a display
- Customers queue to pay before they eat the food – queue may be lengthy, e.g. at lunchtime
- Food can be eaten in the place or taken away

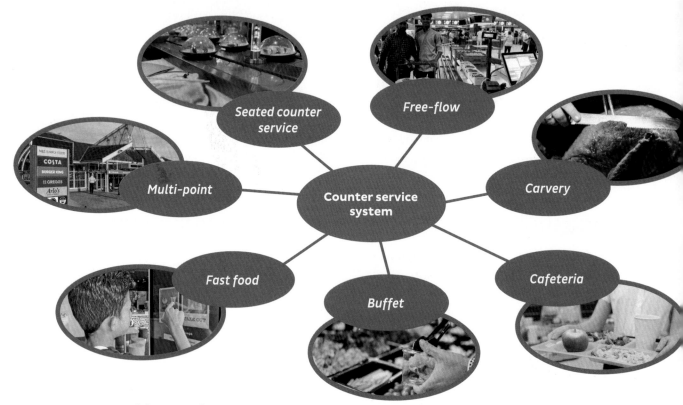

Table service

- Waiting staff take food orders and serve customers seated at a table
- Large restaurants divide tables into areas called stations
- Banquets, wedding receptions, etc. – guests are served by teams of waiting staff
- Food is more expensive in order to pay the wages of the waiting staff
- Gueridon system (trolley / moveable service)
  - Cooking / preparing food at the table to entertain customers

Food being flambéed by the waiter

Transport catering

Careful planning is needed to make sure that:

- Food is kept safe to eat
- Different customer needs are catered for

Trains

- Restaurant carriages on some long-distance trains
- Takeaway cafeteria or trolley service available

Aeroplanes

- Frozen or cook-chilled meals provided on long-distance flights – heated by microwaves
- Trolley drink and snack service available on many short-distance flights

Ships

- Cruise ships provide a variety of food service options
- Ferries usually have a cafeteria service

Food trolley service on a Japanese train

Vending system

- Vending machines sell hot and cold meals, snacks and drinks in a variety of places
- A team of people is needed to service them and maintain their stocks

The commercial (£) sector of the H&C industry

Book link
pp11–12

What do you need to know?

- Types of H&C places that provide services for different customers
- Types of services provided
- Job roles

Commercial sector H&C businesses aim to make a profit.

They can be places where people stay in the accommodation provided (residential).

They can be places where H&C services are provided, but there is no accommodation for people to stay in (non-residential).

Residential commercial sector

Places	Customers	H&C services	Job roles
• Hotels • Guest houses • Bed and breakfast • Inns • Pubs • Farmhouses • Holiday camps and parks • Glamping (luxury camping) • Cruise ships • Long-distance trains • Airlines • Motorway services • Youth hostels	Individuals and groups for: • Business conferences and meetings • Family events • Guests at a social event • Tourists • Participants in leisure activities • Student field trips • Travellers breaking a journey • Passengers on a journey	• Accommodation • Housekeeping • Turn down bed • Room food and drink service • Packed lunches • Formal meals • Study and training facilities • Conference rooms • Internet access • Transport catering service	• Managers • Administrators • Receptionists • Porters • Security • Kitchen brigade • Waiting staff • Barista • Bartender • Housekeeping • Room attendant • Maintenance staff • Conference staff

Non-residential commercial sector

Places

- Restaurants
- Bistros, cafes
- Dining rooms
- Canteens
- Tearooms, coffee shops
- Takeaway and fast food outlets
- Pubs, bars
- Clubs
- Casinos
- Street food
- Pop-up restaurants
- Mobile/roadside food vans
- Motorway services
- Visitor and tourist attractions (theme parks, museums, zoos, etc.)
- Sport stadiums
- Concert/gig venues

Customers

- Individuals/families/groups of different ages
- Tourists
- Visitors
- Workers on regular hours and shift workers

H&C services

- Eat in or takeaway food and drinks
- Private rooms for business or celebrations
- Training facilities
- Meeting rooms
- Internet access

Job roles

- Managers
- Administrators
- Security
- Kitchen brigade
- Receptionist
- Waiting staff
- Barista
- Bartender
- Housekeeping
- Maintenance staff

The non-commercial sector

Book link pp13–14

What do you need to know?

- Types of H&C establishments that provide services for different clients
- Services provided
- Job roles

Non-commercial sector H&C businesses are non-profit making.

They can be places where people stay in the accommodation provided (residential).

They can be places where H&C services are provided, but there is no accommodation for people to stay in (non-residential).

Residential non-commercial sector

Establishments

1. Health and welfare:
   - NHS hospitals
   - NHS nursing and care homes
   - Emergency services
   - Prisons
2. Education:
   - Colleges/universities
   - Boarding schools
3. Armed forces:
   - Army/Navy/Air Force
4. Other:
   - Hostels/shelters
   - Private nursing and care homes

Clients

1. Staff/patients/elderly people/disabled people/mental health patients/visitors/prisoners
2. Students/school children/visitors/staff
3. Armed forces personnel (all ranks)
   Special events visitors
4. Homeless people/people with personal problems/staff
   Elderly, disabled and people with mental health issues/staff

Job roles

- Managers
- Administrators
- Receptionists
- Porters
- Security
- Kitchen brigade
- Food counter staff
- Housekeeping/maintenance staff
- Volunteers

H&C services

- Accommodation
- Food and drinks throughout day and night

Non-residential non-commercial sector

Establishments

1. Workforce catering:
   - Canteens
   - Dining rooms in factories, construction sites, shops, etc.
2. Voluntary sector/Health & welfare:
   - Senior citizen luncheon clubs
   - Charity food vans and cafes
   - Day-care centres
3. Education:
   - Childcare day nurseries
   - School holiday clubs
4. Public sector catering:
   - Schools

Clients

1. Staff from all levels and departments
2. Elderly, disabled, homeless people and those with mental health issues
3. Babies, pre-school and school-age children and teenagers
4. School-age children, teenagers, staff

H&C services

- Food and drinks

Job roles

- Managers
- Administrators
- Porters
- Security
- Receptionist
- Kitchen brigade
- Food counter staff
- Dining room manager
- Maintenance staff
- Volunteers

Job roles in the H&C industry

Book link pp14–17

What do you need to know?
- The different types of jobs in the H&C industry

Managers

Examples in a hotel:
General Manager
Finance Manager
Sales and Bookings Manager
Head Receptionist
Human Resources (staff) Manager
Restaurant Manager
Conference Manager
Head (Executive) Chef
Head Housekeeper

What are they responsible for?
The smooth running of the business
Finances
Security
Employment/dismissal of staff
Staff training and development
Customer satisfaction
Business development and planning
Health, safety and welfare of customers and staff
Cleaning and maintenance of buildings
Making sure the business follows health, safety and employment laws
Sorting out problems and complaints

Administrators

Examples in a hotel:
Secretaries
Assistant/Deputy Managers
Accountant
Cashier

What are they responsible for?
The smooth running of the business
Organising the Manager's diary
Sending letters and emails, making phone calls
Typing, filing, organising staff and customer details, bookings, taxation, etc.
Ordering and paying for supplies, e.g. cleaning materials, food, drinks
Managing events
Organising ITC support

Front of house staff

Examples in a hotel:
Receptionists
Waiting staff
Valets (park car for customer) and Drivers
Bartenders
Cashier
Concierge (assists guests/customers)

What are they responsible for?
Representing and promoting the business
Working directly with customers and back of house staff
Taking bookings
Checking customers in and out of the building
Dealing with customer questions and problems
Assisting customers to their rooms
Setting up meeting rooms

Back of house staff

Examples in a hotel:
Stockroom Manager
Kitchen brigade (all the people who work in a kitchen – see below)
Maintenance team
Gardeners/Groundskeeper
Security guards
Cleaners
Guest room attendants

What are they responsible for?
Buying and organising supplies
Storing, preparing and cooking food
Storing and organising drinks
Ensuring all areas of the buildings (premises) are regularly cleaned, tidy, safe, comfortable and pleasant
Ensuring all areas of the place (inside and outside) are well maintained and working properly
Maintaining security

In each sector of the Hospitality and Catering industry, the jobs are put into an order (called a **hierarchy**), according to the number of people and activities each role is responsible for. The person at the top of the hierarchy has the most responsibilities. For example, in a restaurant/catering kitchen, the Head Chef is at the top and has responsibility for:

- The activities, behaviour and welfare of all the people who work in the kitchen
- Hiring new staff
- Planning and writing the menu
- Choosing, buying and storing the food
- Food hygiene and safety
- Personal safety
- The equipment
- The production of the food
- Managing the costs of running the kitchen
- Organising and maintaining the kitchen

The hierarchy in a catering kitchen is called the **kitchen brigade**.
On the next page, the kitchen brigade is shown in detail.

Head chef
Sous chef
Station chefs
Relief chef
Commis (trainee) chef
Food runner
Kitchen porters

The hierarchy in a catering kitchen

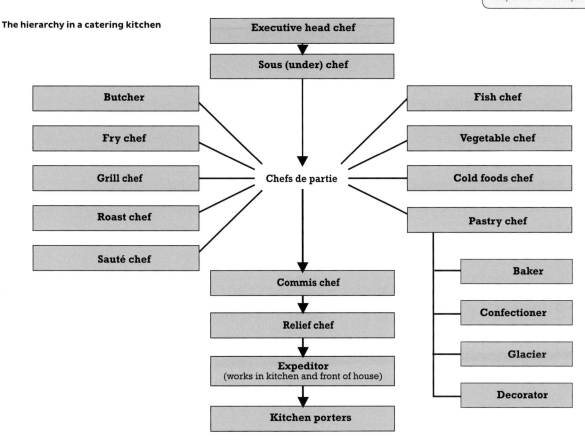

Activity 1.1

Match each job role/responsibility to the right member of staff in a hotel:

Job role/responsibility

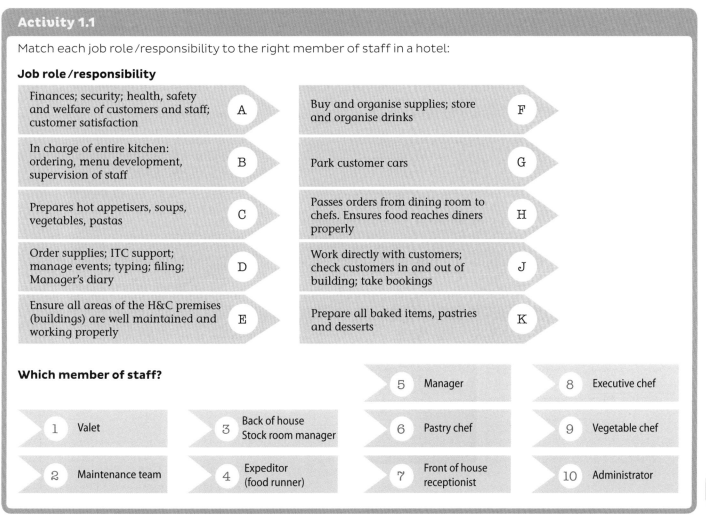

Finances; security; health, safety and welfare of customers and staff; customer satisfaction — A

In charge of entire kitchen: ordering, menu development, supervision of staff — B

Prepares hot appetisers, soups, vegetables, pastas — C

Order supplies; ITC support; manage events; typing; filing; Manager's diary — D

Ensure all areas of the H&C premises (buildings) are well maintained and working properly — E

Buy and organise supplies; store and organise drinks — F

Park customer cars — G

Passes orders from dining room to chefs. Ensures food reaches diners properly — H

Work directly with customers; check customers in and out of building; take bookings — J

Prepare all baked items, pastries and desserts — K

Which member of staff?

1 Valet
2 Maintenance team
3 Back of house Stock room manager
4 Expeditor (food runner)
5 Manager
6 Pastry chef
7 Front of house receptionist
8 Executive chef
9 Vegetable chef
10 Administrator

H&C standards and ratings

Book link
pp18–20

What do you need to know?

- A H&C business with a high rating will attract more customers
- Ratings give customers an assurance of a high standard of service
- Ratings are given for Hotels and guest houses, Restaurants, Food hygiene, Environmental sustainability

Hotels and guest houses

Who does the inspections?	Type of rating awarded	What is being inspected?
Organisations, e.g.: AA/RAC Tourist Boards Visit Britain **Social media, e.g.:** Facebook Twitter TripAdvisor Google Booking.com	Stars: ★ ★★ ★★★ ★★★★ ★★★★★	Open all year? Number of guest rooms Ensuite facilities? Reception facilities Customer care Environment (noisy? quiet?, friendly? relaxing?, clean?) Facilities for disabled people? Staff Catering standards Insurance cover Healthy and safety Security Maintenance of facilities Extra facilities, e.g. gym, swimming pool Internet availability, TV, etc. Car parking Licence for sale of alcohol?

Restaurants

Who does the inspections?	Type of rating awarded	What is being inspected?
Organisations, e.g.: AA The Good Food Guide Michelin Guide	AA: 1–5 rosettes The Good Food Guide: Score between 1 and 10 Michelin Guide: 1, 2, or 3 stars	Type/range of food Quality of food and ingredients Where food comes from (provenance) Standard of cooking, flavour, presentation, quality How skilful and creative the chefs are

Food hygiene

Who does the inspections?	Type of rating awarded	What is being inspected?
Organisations, e.g.: Food Standards Agency and Local Authorities in England, Wales and Northern Ireland Food Hygiene Information Scheme in Scotland Environmental Health officers	Food Hygiene Rating 0–5 	How hygienically the food is handled during preparation, cooking, reheating, cooling, storage, presentation Cleanliness and condition of kitchen and buildings Pest control Ventilation Hand washing and toilet facilities for staff Training of staff in food safety How food safety is managed – HACCP (see page 77)

Environmental sustainability

Who does the inspections?	Type of rating awarded	What is being inspected?
Organisations, e.g.: The Sustainable Restaurant Association	Percentage (%) score for how much they meet the 10 standards set: Less than 50% = 1 star 50–69% = 2 stars More than 70% = 3 stars	Ten standards: 1–4: Where food is sourced: • Locally? • Less meat and dairy foods – more plant foods? • Sustainably caught fish? • Support for farmers and fair trade? 5–6: People: • Are employees treated equally and fairly? • Can employees develop their skills? • How involved is the business in the local community? 7 – 10: Care of environment: • Healthy, balanced meals produced? Energy-efficient equipment used? • Water not wasted? • Food waste reduced? • Material recycled where possible?

Knowledge check – can you remember....?

1. What hospitality means?
2. What catering means?
3. Five types of place where hospitality is provided?
4. Five types of place where catering is provided?
5. Five types of things that suppliers provide the H&C industry with?
6. Three different ways in which food is served to customers in different places?
7. Three H&C services provided by residential commercial businesses?
8. Three H&C services provided by non-residential commercial businesses?
9. Two H&C services provided by residential non-commercial businesses?
10. One H&C service provided by non-residential non-commercial businesses?
11. Three things that a manager in a H&C business is responsible for?
12. Three things that a waiter in a H&C business is responsible for?
13. Two things that a head chef in a H&C business is responsible for?
14. Two things that a stockroom manager in a H&C business is responsible for?
15. Five types of station chefs in the kitchen brigade?
16. Three things that are inspected in hotels and guest houses when giving them a rating?
17. Three things that are inspected in restaurants when giving them a rating?
18. Three things that are inspected during food hygiene checks in catering businesses when giving them a rating?
19. Two things that are inspected during environmental sustainability checks in catering businesses when giving them a rating?
20. Why it is good for a H&C business to be given a high rating?

E-assessment practice questions

Short answer questions

1. Hospitality and catering businesses provide a range of services.
   List four services provided by each of the following:
   a) A large inner-city hotel *[4 marks]*
   b) A family holiday park *[4 marks]*
   c) A cruise ship *[4 marks]*

2. Food is served to customers in a variety of different food service systems.
   Describe how customers receive their food in the following systems:
   a) Cafeteria *[2 marks]*
   b) Buffet service *[2 marks]*
   c) Table service *[2 marks]*
   d) Seated counter service *[2 marks]*

Stretch and challenge question

A restaurant has been taken over by a new management team. The restaurant is located in the centre of a small country town that attracts many tourists. It has previously received only average ratings for its food, customer service and food hygiene standards.

The new management want to improve these ratings and also include ratings for environmental sustainability.

Suggest a variety of ways in which the management could help the restaurant to score high ratings for:
a) The food they offer *[4 marks]*
b) Food hygiene standards *[4 marks]*
c) Customer service *[4 marks]*
d) Environmental sustainability *[4 marks]*

Job requirements and working conditions in the Hospitality and Catering industry

Chapter 2

What do you need to know?

- What is needed for different jobs in the H&C industry **AC1.2**
- Working conditions in the H&C industry **AC1.3**

Book link
pp22–27

LO1 Understand the environment in which hospitality and catering providers operate

Key learning

There are many different types of jobs in the H&C industry.

There are lots of opportunities for people who are willing to work to build a career.

At busy times of the year, (e.g. summer holiday season, Christmas and New Year), the H&C industry hires seasonal **workers**.

Many H&C workers come from different countries around the world.

You can train to get a job in the H&C industry by:

- Doing some work experience
- Going to college when you leave school to take a course
- Working and training as an apprentice.

What type of person do you need to be to work successfully in the H&C industry?

Book link
p24

(What *personal attributes* do you need to have?)

Key terms you should try to include in your answers

Employee – someone who works in the industry and has an employment contract

Employer – someone who owns a business and pays an employee to work there

Worker – someone who works in the industry but does not have an employment contract

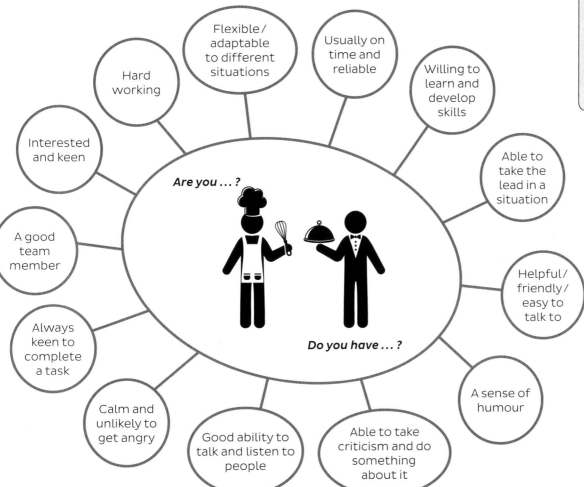

Hard working · Flexible/adaptable to different situations · Usually on time and reliable · Willing to learn and develop skills · Interested and keen · Able to take the lead in a situation · A good team member · Helpful/friendly/easy to talk to · Always keen to complete a task · A sense of humour · Calm and unlikely to get angry · Good ability to talk and listen to people · Able to take criticism and do something about it

Are you ...?

Do you have ...?

What do you need to be able to do and know for different jobs?

Book link
p25

(What skills and knowledge do you need to work in the H&C industry?)

Here are some examples:

	What does a person need to be able to do and know for this job (which skills and knowledge should they have)?

Hotel receptionist

A hotel receptionist needs to have:
- Good personal communication and customer service skills
- Good computer skills
- Good local knowledge to answer customer questions and provide advice and information
- Good knowledge of the business and how it is run
- Good organisational skills

A hotel receptionist needs to be able to:
- Do more than one thing at a time (multi-task)
- Deal with any problems that happen

Chef in a restaurant

A chef needs to have:
- A wide range of good practical cookery skills
- Good knowledge of food
- Good knowledge of food safety and hygiene
- Good organisational skills

A chef needs to be able to:
- Present food creatively
- Use a variety of tools and equipment
- Multi-task

Barista in a busy coffee bar

A barista needs to have:
- A good knowledge of coffee and other drinks
- A good knowledge of food safety and hygiene
- Good organisational skills

A barista needs to be able to:
- Present drinks creatively
- Use a variety of tools and equipment
- Multi-task

Stock room manager in a large kitchen

A stock room manager needs to have:
- Good computer skills
- A good knowledge of food safety and hygiene
- Good organisational skills

Activity 2.1

Fill in the chart to show which skills and knowledge you think each of the following **employees** in the Hospitality and Catering industry needs.

Job role in the H&C industry	What does a person need to be able to do and know for this job (which skills and knowledge should they have)?
A maintenance team member 	*A maintenance team member needs to have:* *A maintenance team member needs to be able to:*
A hotel housekeeping team member 	*A housekeeping team member needs to have:* *A housekeeping team member needs to be able to:*
A restaurant waiter 	*A restaurant waiter needs to have:* *A restaurant waiter needs to be able to:*
A hotel concierge 	*A hotel concierge needs to have:* *A hotel concierge needs to be able to:*

What are the working conditions in the H&C industry?

 Book link
pp26–27

There are rules and laws about how people work:

Rule	Which law?	What does it mean?
Number of working hours in a week	Working Time Directive	People cannot be expected to work for more than 48 hours a week (people can choose to work longer if they want)
Age	Working Time Directive	People under 18 years cannot work more than 8 hours a day, or 40 hours a week
Days off/rest breaks	Working Time Directive	People must have one day off work each week. If they work 6 or more hours a day, they must have a rest break of at least 20 minutes.
How much money people earn	National Minimum Wage	This is the minimum amount you are paid each hour, for most workers over school leaving age.
	National Living Wage	The minimum amount all working people aged 25 years and over should earn.

There are different types of employment contracts:

Type of contract	Hours/start and end times	Sick pay?	Holiday pay?
Full-time – permanent employee	Written down in the contract	Yes	Yes
Part-time – permanent employee	Written down in the contract	Yes – but reduced amount	Yes – but reduced amount
Casual worker – contract from an agency	Vary according to what is needed	No	No
Zero-hours worker	No set hours or times – a worker may or may not accept work offered to them by an **employer**	No	No

There are **extra payments** that people may earn:

Tips – money given to someone by a customer to say thank you for good service (tips may be shared out between staff).

Service charges – an amount of money added to a customer's bill to reward the employees who have given the customer a good service.

Bonus payment – given by some employers to reward their staff for their hard work during the year and helping to make a business successful.

Knowledge check – can you remember....?

1. What a seasonal worker is?

2. Five things (personal attributes) a person needs to be /have to work successfully in the H&C industry?

3. Three types of skill/knowledge a hotel receptionist needs?

4. Three types of skill/knowledge a chef needs?

5. Three types of skill/knowledge a barista needs?

6. Three types of skill/knowledge a kitchen stockroom manager needs?

7. The maximum numbers of hours a week a person can be expected to work?

8. What the National Minimum Wage means?

9. What a tip is?

10. What a service charge is?

E-assessment practice questions

Short answer questions

1. There are many different types of jobs in the Hospitality and Catering industry.
   a) List four personal attributes that someone needs (what type of person they need to be) to be able to work successfully in the Hospitality and Catering industry *[4 marks]*
   b) List three things a person needs to be able to do or know for each of the following jobs:
      i)   Head chef *[3 marks]*
      ii) Front of house manager in a hotel restaurant *[3 marks]*
      iii) Night porter in an inner-city hotel *[3 marks]*

2. There are rules and laws about how people work in the Hospitality and Catering industry.
   What does the law say about each of the following?
   a) How many hours people under 18 years of age can work? *[2 marks]*
   b) How many days off and rest breaks people must be given? *[2 marks]*
   c) What does the National Living Wage mean to people over 25 years old? *[1 mark]*

Chapter 3

Book link
pp28–39

LO1 Understand the environment in which hospitality and catering providers operate

Factors affecting the success of hospitality and catering providers

What do you need to know? **AC1.4**

- The factors that affect the success of a H&C business

Key learning

The success of a H&C business is affected by:

Money – what it costs to run the business and how much money it makes (profit).

Employees – do they work well together to help the business be successful? Are they well trained and happy?

Customer service and satisfaction – do customers like the service they get? Do they come back again?

Trends – is the business keeping up to date and always trying to improve what it does?

Competition – are there similar businesses nearby who compete for customers?

Money

Book link
pp29–31

To run a H&C business, money is needed for many things including:

Food/ingredients

Equipment

Health and safety

Staff wages, pensions and National Insurance payments

Cleaning materials and equipment

Waste and waste disposal

Pest control

Administration (paperwork): insurance, licences, printing, advertising, phone bills, taxes, ITC support, etc.

Heating, lighting, gas supply

Maintenance work, gardening, decorating

Breakages and repairs

Making a profit

To successfully continue in business, it is important to make a profit.

A **profit** is the amount of money made from selling something, after all the costs of making and serving it to customers have been taken out.

For example, in a restaurant, the profit for a menu item is worked out like this:

Menu item:

Fried haddock and chips, served with mushy peas

Cost of ingredients: £2.25

How much customers pay for it: £11.95

Gross profit: £9.70 (£11.95 minus £2.25 for ingredients)

Net profit: the profit made after all the other costs of running a restaurant have been taken out = £0.40 (£9.70 minus £9.30 costs) for each serving of fried haddock and chips with mushy peas sold.

The amount of profit that a H&C business makes is affected by a variety of things:

> **Key terms you should try to include in your answers**
>
> **Gross profit** – the difference between how much the ingredients in a menu item cost and how much it is sold for
>
> **Net profit** – the profit made once all the costs of running a restaurant have been taken out

What affects how much profit is made?	Why does it affect the amount of profit made?
Ordering ingredients and materials	Ordering the right amounts prevents wastage and loss of profits
Wastage	Wasted ingredients and materials have to be paid for, so the money they cost to buy is lost if they are thrown away
A trained and skilled workforce	Trained and skilled workers are less likely to waste ingredients or materials
Popular menu choices	Customers will buy these menu items, so that the food used to make them will not be wasted
The range of services provided	Some services cost more than others to provide

What affects how much profit is made?	Why does it affect the amount of profit made?
Breakages and repairs	Breakages have to be replaced or repaired; both of which cost money
Planning for events	Carefully planned events are less likely to lose money than badly planned events
Feedback/reviews from customers	Good feedback and reviews will encourage new and returning customers to use the business
How well the economy of the country is doing	If the country's economy is struggling, people have less money to spend, fewer tourists visit and spend money and the cost of things such as electricity and gas, food and materials may increase. This can all affect the amount of profit a business can make.

Customer service and satisfaction

Book link pp35–36

Good customer service skills and satisfaction are an essential part of the image and success of a H&C business, and they should be of a high standard in all of the services the business provides. If customers are happy and satisfied with the service they have received, they will tell other people about it and recommend the business to them. They are also likely to come back and become regular customers.

What makes a customer in a hotel or restaurant happy?

A business that provides a quick and well-run service

A business that takes action on customer feedback

Staff who listen to customers and answer their questions

Staff who understand customers' needs and wants

A business that provides what customers expect

Staff who are well trained, helpful, cheerful, smiling and friendly

Staff who aim to solve customer complaints promptly and politely

Trends

Book link p37

A **trend** means the ways in which something is developing or changing and becoming well known and/or popular. H&C businesses should be aware of and keep up with trends which will affect their success. An example of a trend which continues to affect the success of businesses in all industries is **information and computer technology**, and there are some important trends that are designed to attract customers and improve their experience of it:

Satellite technology and beacons – these show people on their mobile phones their location or the directions to another location. They are also used by businesses to:

- Find would-be customers and show them nearby restaurants, hotels, bars, etc.
- Give them links to the services provided so they can choose what to eat or drink.

Customer Relationship Management systems (CRMs) – these enable customers to make online bookings, order food and drinks, etc., directly to a H&C business. A restaurant, for example, then knows how many customers are expected and can manage its kitchen, ordering and customer needs more efficiently.

Social media – this enables businesses to receive feedback (good and bad!) from customers who write reviews and send photographs or videos of their experiences to other people.

Smart devices linked to smartphones – devices such as smart watches linked to smartphones use apps to monitor things and allow people to send requests or instructions to other devices. H&C businesses are using this technology to enable customers to:

- Place orders for food, etc., when they are elsewhere
- Check in to hotels online
- Unlock their hotel room door with a smart watch or similar device
- Control their TV, hotel room heating, lighting, etc.

Environmental sustainability

Book link
pp31–33

Another trend that affects the success of H&C businesses is environmental sustainability. Research shows that the following things all have a big impact on the environment:

- Food production (especially meat, poultry, eggs and dairy foods)
- The production and use of packaging materials (especially plastics)
- Refrigeration and food transport (especially using lorries, ships and aeroplanes).

In order to reduce their impact on the environment, help save money, save space and give them a good reputation with their customers, many H&C businesses are being encouraged to become more **environmentally sustainable** by doing things such as:

- Using renewable energy, e.g. solar from solar panels
- Using automatic switches to control lighting and air conditioning
- Using water-saving washing machines and dishwashers
- Reducing, re-using and recycling any waste they create by doing the following things.

Reducing the use of:

- **Food packaging**
  - Buying food with minimum amounts of packaging
  - Buying food with biodegradable packaging that will naturally break down in the soil
  - Not using individual sachets /packets of sauces, sugar, butter, etc.
- **Food waste**
  - Reducing portion sizes served to customers
  - Providing containers for customers to take left-over food home to eat later
  - Passing on good quality left-over foods to food charities to make into meals for people who do not have enough money for all the food they need
  - Turning food waste into compost to grow vegetables and herbs
  - Making stock from vegetable peelings and off-cuts and poultry and meat bones
  - Storing food correctly so that it is not wasted.
- **Disposable items**
  - Not using disposable plastic cutlery and drinking straws
  - Not using paper or plastic plates, dishes, serviettes, tablecloths, etc.

Re-using:

- **Left-over foods** to make new dishes, e.g. left-over vegetables can be turned into soups; left-over cooked meat can be used in pies
- **Packaging and containers** – some are re-usable. Some empty containers can be used to store other ingredients (they must be clearly labelled to say what is in them).

Recycling:

- Left-over used **cooking oil** can be recycled into biofuel to run machines and vehicles
- Many plastics, glass, aluminium foil, paper and card can be recycled
- Products made from **recycled materials** can be bought and used, e.g.:
  - Paper hand towels and toilet rolls from recycled paper
  - Plastic chairs and containers from recycled plastics
  - Bottles and glasses from recycled glass.

Recycled paper products   Recycled plastic chairs   Recycled drinking glasses

Competition with other businesses

Book link p36

There is a lot of competition between H&C businesses to attract and keep regular customers. The chart below shows some of the ideas that H&C businesses can try in order to keep up with the competition from other businesses:

What does the H&C business want to do?	Examples of products and services that could be offered to help the H&C business be successful	How a H&C business can show would-be customers that it is a good choice for them

Offer a range of different products and services to attract customers and compete with other similar local businesses	Wedding fairs, ceremonies and receptions
	
	Birthday and celebration parties (e.g. bar/bat mitzvahs, wedding anniversaries, company dinner and dances)
	
	School and college proms
	
	University graduation ceremonies
	
	Conferences and training courses
	
	Quiz nights and other competitions
	
	Special food events, e.g. curry nights; Christmas meals; food, beer and wine festivals
	
	Craft fairs and other community events
	
	Special sports events viewing and celebrations, e.g. national and international rugby games, world athletics events, etc.
	
	Offer a range of catering services, menus and cultural food events
		The business _should_:
		Reply to customer enquiries and give them a price quote within 24 hours
		Make sure the business has a detailed, reliable, user-friendly and regularly updated website
		Carry out market research to find out the number and types of other businesses that it will compete with
		Find out about the local population:
		  – How many people are there?
		  – What are their age groups?
		  – What are their lifestyles?
		  – What are their needs and wants?
		
		The business _could_:
		Advertise in different ways and places, using good-quality images and clear explanations of the services on offer and the prices
		Offer competitive prices, group discounts, customer loyalty schemes (e.g. collect tokens to earn a free meal)
		Offer meal deals, e.g. discounts for pensioners, free bottle of wine with a meal, buy two meals and get a third one free
		Offer competitive/discounted accommodation for guests

Customer needs and wants

Book link
p36

There are different groups of people who use the services that H&C businesses provide. The chart below shows that each group has different needs and wants, and a successful business will provide services for these in order to attract customers.

Type of customer	Examples of their needs and wants	Examples of how a H&C business can provide for their needs and wants
Couples and small groups who want a leisure visit for two or three days	Short leisure breaks Reasonably priced accommodation	Special hotel 'packages' at quiet times of year, e.g. 'out of [holiday] season' or in the winter, offering reduced price accommodation and including one or two evening meals as well as breakfast
	Leisure facilities	Swimming pool, gym, beauty therapy, spa
Families with young children	Value for money	Inexpensive restaurant that has a children's menu
	Suitable accommodation and facilities	Cots, small beds, highchairs, en suite toilet, shower and bath
	Activities	Outdoor / indoor play area, games, swimming pool
Business customers	Suitable accommodation for meetings	Meeting places / conference rooms
	Computer technology	Smart screens to show films and presentations, Internet access throughout, video conferencing facilities, smartphone charging points
	Catering	Business lunches, refreshments available throughout the day
Travellers / tourists	Suitable, reasonably priced accommodation	Single / double rooms, dormitories (large room containing beds for numerous people); en suite toilet, shower and bath; space to store bicycles, walking boots, body boards, etc.; laundry services
	Activities	Arrange local tours, walks, theatre trips, etc.; swimming pool, gym, beauty therapy, spa
	Flexible availability of food	Packed breakfasts and lunches; hot food and drinks available out of set mealtimes; vending machines selling snacks and drinks
Millennials (people born from 1980 to 2000), who have a big influence on the H&C industry	To eat 'on the go' To eat locally produced, healthy, fresh food	Packed breakfasts and lunches; hot food and drinks available out of set mealtimes; vending machines selling snacks and drinks
	Use all types of social media, digital and computer technologies	Internet access throughout; smartphone charging points
	Environmentally sustainable services and products	Minimal use of plastics; recycling bins, etc., in use; provide food that is mainly plant based and has been produced sustainably; use biodegradable products such as cleaning products and paper drinking straws
	High-quality and contemporary (modern) products and services, e.g. to book and use services through a mobile phone at their own convenience	Provide exciting, well-designed, user-friendly social spaces to meet with friends, with computer technology available throughout

Policies, laws and regulations

Book link
pp37–38

Policies, laws and regulations are made by the government, and many of these affect the success of H&C businesses, including:

Licensing laws for selling alcohol – what they cover:

- A H&C business must have a licence to sell alcohol
- Alcohol can only be sold at certain times of the day
- Alcohol can only be sold to people who are 18 years old or older.

Employment laws – what they cover:

- Health and safety regulations
- Pension and National Insurance contributions
- Working hours and holiday entitlement
- Gender, age, religious, disability and racial anti-discrimination laws
- Income Tax and insurance
- Child care
- Sick pay
- Redundancy and dismissal
- Employment contracts
- Trade unions
- Employment of overseas workers.

Health and safety (customers and workers) laws – what they cover:

- Fire regulations – to avoid fires starting and to make sure people can escape from a burning building
- Building regulations – to make sure all electrical switches and equipment are safe to use
- Use and storage of chemicals, e.g. for cleaning and maintenance
- Tobacco and e-cigarette smoking regulations
- Food Safety Act and other regulations to make sure that food and drinks are safe to consume
- Public liability insurance cover to claim from if there is an accident.

Tax collection laws – what they cover:

- Income Tax – paid by employees to the government
- Value Added Tax (VAT) – collected by businesses from goods and services that customers buy; sent to the government.

Businesses need to:

- Be aware of all the regulations and laws that will affect them
- Make sure that they have the appropriate checks carried out and up-to-date certificates to prove that they have complied with the law.

If it is proved that a business has not obeyed laws or regulations, it can be prosecuted and made to pay a large fine (money) or have an aspect of its licence to trade taken away. This will seriously affect its reputation and profits.

Media

Book link
p39

It is important for H&C businesses to advertise and promote their products and services by using social media, television and films, magazines and other printed media.

Social media is used by millions of businesses and followed by billions of people across the world. It can have positive and negative effects on the success of a H&C business.

Positive effects of social media on H&C businesses	Negative effects of social media on H&C businesses
A very large number of customers (a customer base) can be contacted.	H&C employees who use social media may say something negative about the business, which will rapidly reach many people through re-tweets, comments, likes and shares. This may damage its reputation (and the employee may lose their job!).
Specific customer groups can be targeted with advertisements and special offers, e.g. young adults, families with young children, business customers.	Negative feedback and complaints from customers about the service they have received will reach a lot of people who may then decide not to use the business.
Customers feel they have a personal connection with a business, which many people like. They are more likely to trust the business.	If messages and statements (e.g. confidential information about the business) are sent by mistake on social media, they will spread very rapidly and are almost impossible to put right.

Knowledge check – can you remember....?

1. Three things that affect the success of a H&C business?
2. Five things that a H&C business needs money for?
3. What a gross profit is?
4. What a net profit is?
5. Five things that affect how much profit a H&C business makes?
6. Four things that make hotel or restaurant customers happy?
7. Two trends in computer technology that will attract customers to a restaurant?
8. Two ways in which H&C businesses can become more environmentally sustainable?
9. Two ways in which H&C businesses can reduce their use of food packaging?
10. Two ways in which H&C businesses can reduce food waste?
11. Two ways in which H&C businesses can reduce their use of plastics?
12. Two products made from recycled materials that a H&C business could use?
13. Four products/services that a H&C business could offer to help make it successful?
14. Three things a H&C business *should* do to help make it successful?
15. Three things a H&C business *could* do to help make it successful?
16. Two needs and wants for *each* of the following groups of people who are customers of a H&C business?
    a) Families with young children
    b) Business customers
    c) Travellers and tourists
    d) Millennials
    e) Couples/small groups of people
17. Two ways in which social media can have a positive effect on H&C businesses?
18. Two ways in which social media can have a negative effect on H&C businesses?

E-assessment practice questions

Short answer questions

1. The amount of profit that a hospitality and catering business makes is affected by a variety of things.

   State one reason why each of the following affects the amount of profit made:
   a) Wasted food *[1 mark]*
   b) Feedback and reviews from customers *[1 mark]*
   c) The range of services provided *[1 mark]*

2. There is a lot of competition between hospitality and catering businesses to attract and keep regular customers.

   Suggest four ways in which a hospitality and catering business can attract people to become regular customers *[4 marks]*

3. There are different groups of people who use the services that hospitality and catering businesses provide.

   For each of the following groups of people, identify two ways in which a hospitality and catering business can provide their needs and wants:
   a) Families with young children *[2 marks]*
   b) Business customers *[2 marks]*
   c) Travellers and tourists *[2 marks]*

Stretch and challenge question

A new bar and restaurant is opening in a city centre in which many people in the millennials age group live and work.

The management want to provide services that will appeal particularly to this group. Suggest three services they could provide, giving details and reasons for your answers. *[4 marks for each suggestion = 12]*

Operational activities in a kitchen

Chapter 4

What do you need to know? **AC2.1**

Why good organisation of a catering kitchen is important for making sure that:

- Good-quality and safe food is made for customers
- Ingredients and equipment are used properly and economically
- Employees work effectively

Book link pp40–51

LO2 Understand how hospitality and catering provisions operate

Key learning

There are **four** main activities that happen in a catering kitchen:

- **Storing** equipment, materials and food
- **Preparing** food ready for cooking
- **Cooking** and presenting food
- **Cleaning** and maintaining the kitchen and equipment.

The kitchen needs to have a suitable layout so that a good **workflow** can be set up.

Good-quality **kitchen equipment**, **ingredients** and **materials** are essential for the efficient and safe production of food.

Food safety is the most important priority in the operation of a catering kitchen.

To make sure the business makes a profit, it is important to have good **stock control**.

It is important to organise and carefully manage all the **paperwork** that is needed in a catering kitchen.

Chefs/cooks working in a catering kitchen must wear clean **protective clothing**.

The **safety and security** of employees in the kitchen is very important.

> ### Key terms you should try to include in your answers
>
> **Materials** – the range of items and products that are needed to run a H&C business, besides equipment and ingredients
>
> **Stock** – the name for all the materials, ingredients and equipment that are in use in a catering kitchen
>
> **Workflow** – the way that food passes through the kitchen from delivery of ingredients to the finished meal served to the customer

Workflow and layout of a catering kitchen

Book link pp40–43

A catering kitchen is divided into areas where different activities take place:

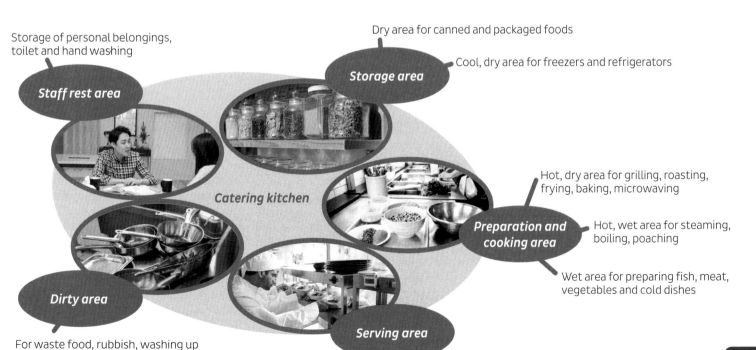

Storage of personal belongings, toilet and hand washing

Staff rest area

Dry area for canned and packaged foods

Cool, dry area for freezers and refrigerators

Storage area

Catering kitchen

Hot, dry area for grilling, roasting, frying, baking, microwaving

Preparation and cooking area

Hot, wet area for steaming, boiling, poaching

Wet area for preparing fish, meat, vegetables and cold dishes

Dirty area

For waste food, rubbish, washing up

Serving area

For plating up and presenting food

The way that food passes through the kitchen from delivery to the customer is called the workflow:

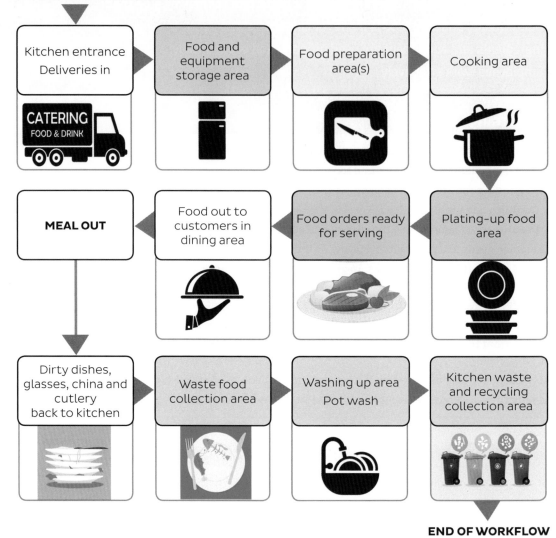

The layout of a catering kitchen

A good catering kitchen should:

- Be easy, pleasant and comfortable to work in
- Have a low risk of cross-contamination by bacteria.

The kitchen should be designed so that:

There is plenty of storage space for food

Equipment, ingredients and water supply are within easy reach for the chefs

It is well lit, not too hot and always has plenty of fresh air

The dirty area is well away from food preparation areas

Steam, fumes and heat are extracted from the kitchen

It is easy to clean and maintain

Here is an example of a kitchen layout for the kitchen of a medium-sized hotel. It shows the workflow and the different areas:

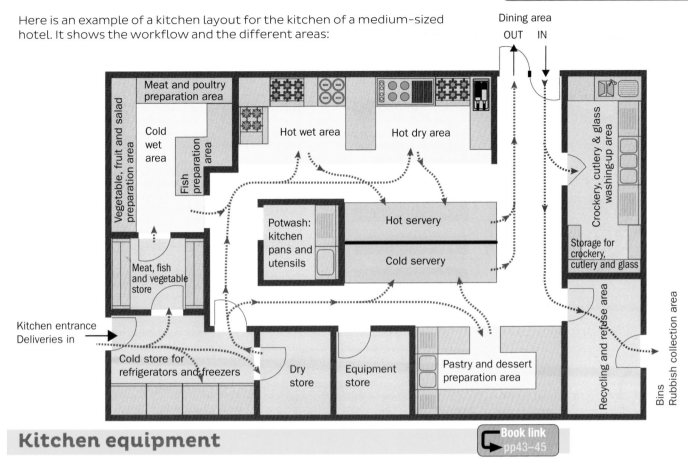

Kitchen equipment

Book link pp43–45

There are five groups of equipment used in a catering kitchen:

Large equipment

E.g. ovens, cooking ranges, walk-in freezers and refrigerators, steamers, grills, floor-standing mixers and processors, deep-fat fryers, blast chiller

Mechanical equipment

E.g. mincer, food processor, mixer, vegetable peeler, dough mixer, dishwasher

Small hand-held utensils and equipment

E.g. bowls, jugs, pans, whisks, spatulas, knives, chopping boards, sieves, food temperature probes, etc.

First aid and safety equipment

E.g. first aid kit, safety and emergency exit signs, fire extinguishers, smoke, gas and carbon monoxide alarms, safety and emergency lighting

Food safety equipment

E.g. colour-coded chopping boards, knives, tongs, food labels, food temperature probe, etc., to prevent cross-contamination

31

Activity 4.1: Food safety equipment

Which board should you use for the following foods?
(Match the correct colour board to the correct foods)

Green	Raw meat and poultry
Yellow	Dairy and bakery
White	Vegetables
Red	Raw fish
Brown	Fruits and salad vegetables
Blue	Cooked meat, poultry and fish

When choosing equipment for a catering kitchen, several points should be considered, including:

The size

Where it will go in the kitchen

How much noise it makes when being used

How easy it is to clean and maintain

How easy it is to use

How safe it is to use

How well it is made

How many different jobs it can do

How much energy / water it uses

How long the manufacturer's warranty lasts

Activity 4.2: Equipment: name the knives

The pictures below show a variety of kitchen knives that are used to prepare different foods.
Match the correct knife to its name and the description of the foods it is designed to be used for:

A

B

C

D

E

1 **Palette knife**: Spreading ingredients and lifting cooked items from a baking tray

2 **Paring or vegetable knife**: Peeling fruits and vegetables

3 **Chef's / cook's knife**: Chopping a variety of foods e.g. vegetables, nuts, chocolate, herbs

4 **Filleting knife**: Filleting fish

5 **Boning knife/meat knife**: Cutting a whole chicken into joints

Materials

Book link
p46

Materials that are used in a catering kitchen include:

Cleaning materials
- Detergents for washing dishes, cutlery etc.
- Detergents for washing clothes, dishcloths, oven gloves, etc.
- Scourers, washing up cloths, floor cloths, mops, dustpans and brushes, brooms, buckets
- Chemicals to clean walls, equipment, toilets and floors

Employee welfare materials
- First aid
- Hand wash liquid
- Paper towels / hand driers
- Toilet paper
- Feminine hygiene disposal bags
- Fire extinguishers and smoke / gas alarms

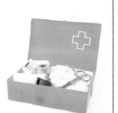

Food preparation materials
- Kitchen paper, foil, baking paper
- Food labels
- Food storage boxes and bags
- Cloths for dishwashing, oven gloves, disposable gloves

Waste disposal materials
- Waste bags and bins
- Recycling bags and bins

Maintenance materials
- Filters for extractors
- Oil for greasing machines
- Light bulbs and batteries

Stock control

Book link
pp46–47

A stock controller works with the catering kitchen, front of house (bar / restaurant), cleaning and maintenance departments in a H&C business to make sure that they have all the stock they need. They often use computer technology to help make their job easier and quicker.

These are the jobs they have to do:

Order ingredients, materials and equipment

Know how much stock has been bought and how much has been used

Keep a list of current prices for all stock

Keep all receipts, delivery notes, emails from suppliers, etc., in order

Store stock (especially food) correctly and use older stock first before new stock (FIFO – First In, First Out)

Make sure there is always enough stock available

Prevent stock being damaged by pests (e.g. insects), water, heat, etc.

Prepare and send out orders for each department in the business

Keep a detailed list of the stock in the business

Paperwork in a catering kitchen

Book link pp48–49

There are many forms and pieces of information that need to be completed, signed and dated, and kept in a catering kitchen. Many of these are required by law, e.g. gas and fire safety certificates, accident reports.

Keeping documents in a well-organised way is important, as it helps to maintain good organisation, the safety of workers and customers, and ensures that bills are paid on time.

- Health and safety documents and certificates
- Staff employment and training information
- Staff health checks, sickness and accident records
- Risk assessment documents
- Stock orders, supplier invoices and delivery notes
- Environmental Health and Trading Standards information documents
- Food safety documents and certificates
- Customer feedback and information
- Events, advertising and media information
- Financial and budget documents

Protective clothing

Book link pp50–51

The cook's /chef's uniform is a well-known symbol of the catering industry.

Wearing the uniform shows that the cook /chef represents a H&C business and is professional, clean and smart.

There are several parts to the uniform. Each part has a special purpose:

Hat

- Protects hair from smoke and oil
- Lets air cool the head
- Stops hair falling in food

Some chefs wear a cotton necktie to absorb sweat.

A long-sleeved, double-breasted, cotton jacket

- Protects body from burns and heat from ovens and grills
- Makes a clean barrier between the chef and the food
- Absorbs sweat

Knee-length cotton apron

- Protects lower body from burns

Patterned or plain cotton trousers

- Comfortable to wear in a hot kitchen

Strong, well-fitting, slip-resistant shoes, with toe protectors and low heels

- Protect feet from burns and falling objects
- Help prevent slips and falls

There are rules about wearing a chef's uniform:

Change into the uniform at work

Do not wear jewellery (plain wedding rings are allowed)

Change the uniform for a clean one every day

Do not wear heavy make-up, false nails, nail varnish or false eyelashes

Wash and iron the uniform regularly

Do not wear strong scents (affects the taste and smell of food)

Do not wear the uniform in public places to prevent contamination by microbes

Wear a hairnet if hair is longer than collar and/or a beard net (if necessary)

Safety and security in the catering kitchen Book link p51

People who work in a catering kitchen need to be aware of possible personal safety and security issues in a kitchen, e.g.:

Possible personal safety issues:

- Risk of fire or electrocution

- Risk of trips, slips and falls

- Risk of injury from machinery, e.g. electric food slicer; steamer

- Risk of cuts, burns and scalds

- Risk of heavy stored items falling from shelves or cupboards

Possible security issues:

- Stealing personal items from staff area
- Stealing equipment, e.g. knives, small electrical items and utensils from the business

- Stealing stored ingredients, alcohol and materials from the business

- Vandalism of buildings (deliberately damaging buildings)

- Arson (deliberately setting fire to a place)

- Problems with alcohol and drug misuse (a big problem in the Hospitality and Catering industry)

Knowledge check – can you remember....?

1. Three main activities that happen in a catering kitchen?
2. What the most important priority is in a catering kitchen?
3. The names of three areas of a catering kitchen and what happens in them?
4. What 'workflow' means?
5. Three important points for the design of a catering kitchen?
6. Four groups of equipment that are used in a catering kitchen?
7. Five points to consider when choosing equipment for a catering kitchen?
8. Three types of materials that are used in a catering kitchen?
9. Three jobs that a stock controller has to do?
10. Four types of information that have to be completed, signed and dated, and kept in a catering kitchen?
11. Two reasons why a chef wears a uniform?
12. Two reasons why a chef should wear a hat?
13. Two reasons why a chef should wear a cotton jacket?
14. One reason why a chef should wear an apron?
15. Two reasons why a chef should wear sturdy, well-fitting shoes?
16. Five rules about wearing a chef's uniform?
17. Three possible safety issues in a catering kitchen?
18. Three possible security issues in a catering kitchen?

E-assessment practice questions

Short answer questions

1. Catering kitchens are divided up in to areas where different activities take place.
   a) List two areas in a catering kitchen and one activity that takes place in each of those two areas *[4 marks]*
   b) Give two reasons why good organisation in a catering kitchen is important *[2 marks]*
   c) List three things that a stock controller has to do in a catering kitchen *[3 marks]*

2. A chef/cook wears a uniform when working in the kitchen, and there are rules about how they should wear it. Give a reason for each of the following rules:
   a) Wear a clean uniform every day *[1 mark]*
   b) Do not wear jewellery *[1 mark]*
   c) Wear a hair or beard net *[1 mark]*

Stretch and challenge questions

An inspection of a hotel kitchen by Environmental Health Officers has revealed the following personal safety and food hygiene problems:

1. Several chefs not following the rules of food hygiene practice
2. Faulty refrigerators that are not keeping food cool enough
3. Evidence of insect and mouse infestation in the kitchen and store rooms
4. Detection of gas leaking from a pipe from one of the cookers
5. Not enough smoke alarms in the kitchen
6. Very few hygiene and safety warning signs displayed in the kitchen
7. Torn vinyl flooring in various places in the kitchen

For each of the problems above, list the documents and pieces of information (e.g. certificates) that hospitality and catering businesses are required to keep and which the Environmental Health Officers will demand to see, to check whether or not the hotel managers have been complying with Health and Safety and Food Safety laws. *[7 marks]*

The operation of the front of house

LO2 Understand how hospitality and catering provisions operate

What do you need to know? AC2.2

Why good organisation of the front of house in a restaurant or hotel reception is important for making sure that:

- Customers are treated well and at a high standard so they feel welcomed and happy
- Customers make the business successful by recommending it to other people and becoming regular customers themselves

Key learning

Front of house means all the areas where customers go in a restaurant: reception, dining area, bar, waiting area, cloakrooms, toilets.

In a hotel, the front of house is the **reception**, where customers are greeted and check in when they arrive, and check out when they leave.

The front of house needs to have a suitable layout so that a good workflow can be set up.

Workflow in a restaurant means how quickly and well meals come from the kitchen and are served to customers, and how drinks are served to them from the bar.

Food safety has a high priority in the operation of the front of house.

The **safety and security** of employees in the front of house is very important.

It is important to organise and carefully manage all the **materials**, **equipment** and **paperwork** that is needed in the front of house.

Front of house staff should wear appropriate clothing, as required by the hospitality and catering business they work for.

Activities in the front of house and where they take place in a restaurant

Book link
p52

Which area?	Activities	Why the activities and the quality of the area are important for the success of the H&C business
 **Entrance / reception area**	To welcome customers and take them to a table. It is important that front of house staff smile and are polite and helpful to customers.	A customer's first impression of a restaurant is really important. • Does it (and the staff who work there) look welcoming, clean and tidy? • Is there a menu to look at before the customer goes into the restaurant? • If the customer is disabled, can they get into the restaurant easily?
 **Waiting area**	A place where customers wait for a table to become ready for them.	The customers will be happy to wait if: • The waiting area is comfortable and welcoming • They are given menus so they can choose their meal • They are offered drinks while they wait.
Bar area	The place where customers have a drink and meet people before they have their meal.	The customers will feel relaxed before they go to their table.

Dining area

Customers are served with their meal.

The dining area is usually divided into sections (called stations).

Each station has one or more waiter(s) who serve customers at a set number of tables. This means that those customers will be served as soon as possible, because the waiter(s) are concentrating only on them and not the whole restaurant.

The dining area should be a place that customers recommend to other people and want to come back to another time. It should:

● Be a comfortable place to sit – not too hot or cold, good chairs, etc.
● Be a pleasant place to be in, e.g. nice decorations, plant/flower displays, background music, pictures on the walls, not too noisy, etc.
● Be away from strong smells and fumes from the kitchen
● Have enough space for customers and for waiting staff to move around freely
● Have a menu that suits people's different needs and wants
● Welcome disabled customers and their guide dog/ assistance dog.

Cloakrooms / toilets

For customers to use to make their stay more comfortable.

Disabled people should be able to use the cloakrooms and toilets easily.

If these are clean and regularly checked, customers will be pleased.

Workflow and layout of the front of house in a restaurant

Book link
pp53–54

In the same way as a catering kitchen, the front of house in a restaurant needs a good workflow, especially when it is busy with lots of customers. Here is an example of the workflow in the front of house of a busy restaurant:

CUSTOMERS COME INTO RESTAURANT ← **END OF WORKFLOW**

Greet customers and take them to a table	Give customers the dessert menu	Take customer orders for desserts and send to kitchen	Re-set table ready for next customers
Give customers a menu	Clear table Take used plates and cutlery to kitchen	Serve desserts	Customers leave restaurant
Take customer orders for drinks and serve them	Check customers are happy with their meal	Clear table Take used dishes and cutlery to kitchen	Take payment for the meal
Take orders for food and send to kitchen	Serve meals to customers	Take orders for coffee and other drinks	Give customers the bill for their meal

The layout of a restaurant

A good restaurant layout should:

- Be easy for staff and customers to move around in – not too many tables and chairs
- Be easy, pleasant and comfortable to work and eat in
- Have clearly signposted emergency exits.

Front of house equipment

Book link
pp55–56

There are seven groups of equipment used in the front of house in a restaurant:

1. Table top

Examples of equipment:

Table covers
Menu holders
Salt and pepper mills
Table signs and numbers
Knives, forks, spoons
Place mats
Glasses

2. Food service

Examples of equipment:

China plates, dishes, serving dishes
Stainless steel bowls and plates
Wooden platters
Cups, saucers
Individual oven-to-table dishes, e.g. pie dish

3. Waiting at table

Examples of equipment:

Trays, tray stands
Serving spoons and tongs
Bottle openers
Customer order notepads and pens
Computer-generated customer ordering equipment, e.g. smart pad or tablet
Candle lighter

4. Customer seating

Examples of equipment:

Chairs, stools
Benches
Picnic tables and benches
High chairs for babies
Booster seats for children
Armchairs and sofas
Sun shades and garden seats

5. Organisation

Examples of equipment:

Rope barriers for queueing
Direction signs
Menu posters and blackboards
Cutlery storage trays
Wine racks and glass holders
Cupboards and drawers

6. First aid and safety

Examples of equipment:

First aid kit
Safety and emergency exit signs
Fire extinguishers
Smoke and gas alarms
Safety lighting

7. Bar area

Examples of equipment:

Drinks measures
Refrigerators
Ice bucket and tongs
Bottle openers
Food blender/juicer
Coffee machine
Panini maker
Frappuccino ice maker (often used in coffee shops)
Glasses
Washing up equipment
Till

Materials

Book link p56

Materials that are used in the front of house in a restaurant include:

Types of materials	Examples	
Cleaning materials	Detergents for cleaning glasses, etc., at the bar Washing up cloths, floor cloths, mops, dustpans and brushes, brooms, buckets, etc., to clean the tables, bar area, floor, toilets and waiting area	
Materials for food service	Serviettes, napkins Packets and pots of sauces, salad dressings, seasonings, sugar, milk, cream, jams, marmalade, butter, vegetable fat spread, etc. Candles and table decorations, e.g. fresh flowers	
Waste disposal materials	Waste bags and bins Recycling bags and bins	
Employee welfare materials	First aid materials Hand wash liquid Paper towels/hand driers Toilet paper Feminine hygiene disposal bags	
Maintenance materials	Replacement filters for extractors, coffee machines, etc. Replacement light bulbs, batteries, till rolls Replacement of broken equipment, e.g. glasses, china plates, etc.	

Stock control

 Book link p57

As with the kitchen, it is necessary for good stock control to take place, especially as the front of house uses expensive products such as wines and spirits. There should be someone who looks after the stock and keeps records of what is bought, what is used and what needs to be re-ordered.

Clothing for the front of house

 Book link p57

The dress code for front of house staff varies, depending on the H&C business.

What the front of house staff wear is important because:

- It gives customers an important first impression – smart-looking staff give a good impression of the business
- A uniform sets a standard and avoids staff working in unsuitable clothes
- It makes the employees feel part of a team
- It makes staff take care and pride in their work
- Customers will know who is a member of staff if they need to ask them something

Activity 5.1: Dress code in the front of house

There are rules about wearing a front of house uniform. Fill in the table below:

Dress code rules in the front of house		Explain why each rule is necessary and important
1. A uniform should be worn by front of house staff		
2. Front of house staff should change into their uniform at their workplace and should not wear their uniform in public areas such as on buses and trains		
3. The uniform should be changed every day and washed and ironed before it is worn again.		
4. False nails, nail polish and false eyelashes should not be worn		
5. Strong scents and after-shave lotions should not be worn		

Safety and security in the front of house

Book link
p58

CCTV camera in a restaurant

People who work in the front of house need to be aware of possible safety and security issues, most of which are the same as in a catering kitchen (see page 35).

There may also be security issues when dealing with possible drunk and/or aggressive customers, or customers who argue with the staff about a problem, e.g. with their bill or the quality of the food.

The management of the business should make sure that staff are trained to deal with problems and that security systems are in place, e.g.:

- Security guards
- Closed-circuit television (CCTV) cameras
- An emergency button to alert the police if there is a problem

Knowledge check – can you remember....?

1. Three main activities that happen in the front of house in a restaurant?

2. Three important points for the design and layout of a restaurant?

3. How the dining area in a restaurant is divided up?

4. Three things that make a dining area a pleasant place to be in?

5. Why it is important that front of house staff smile and are polite and helpful to customers?

6. Five groups of equipment that are used in a restaurant, with three examples for each group?

7. Three types of materials that are used in a restaurant?

8. Three reasons why front of house staff wear a uniform?

9. Four rules about wearing a front of house uniform?

10. Two possible security issues in a restaurant?

E-assessment practice questions

Short answer questions

1. The front of house area in hotels and restaurants is divided up into areas where different activities take place. For each of the following areas, give one activity that takes place and one reason why the quality of the area is important for the success of a H&C business:

   a) Entrance/reception area *[2 marks]*

   b) Bar area *[2 marks]*

   c) Dining area *[3 marks]*

2. The safety and security of the staff and customers are important in the front of house. For each of the following situations, suggest one way in which the management of a H&C business could help to prevent or manage the risks:

   a) A customer in the bar area drinks too much alcohol and starts shouting and behaving in an aggressive manner *[1 mark]*

   b) A customer has their mobile phone stolen while they are eating their meal *[1 mark]*

   c) The fire alarms go off in a restaurant and the customers and staff all have to leave the building by the emergency exits *[1 mark]*

Meeting customer requirements

Chapter 6

What do you need to know? **AC2.3**

- Why it is important for H&C businesses to meet customers' needs and requirements

Book link
pp60–65

LO2 Understand how hospitality and catering provisions operate

Key learning

Customers have a variety of **needs** and **wants** when they visit a H&C business.

Customers **expect** H&C businesses to provide certain services for their customers.

If a H&C business provides the customers' needs and wants well, it will be successful.

A H&C business can find out what customers need and want by doing **market research**, e.g. surveys, online reviews and feedback, talking to customers, reading industry magazines and searching the Internet.

Customers have certain **legal rights** when they use a H&C business.

Customer needs, wants and expectations

Book link
p60

There are three levels for what customers need, want and expect from a H&C business:

1. Essential: things that a customer would expect to be provided by a restaurant or hotel, e.g.:

In a restaurant

A variety of menu choices

Information about the ingredients used (e.g. for people with food allergies)

Toilets and hand washing facilities

Access and facilities for disabled people

Internet availability

In a hotel

A bar or vending machine serving hot and cold drinks

Food available at different times of day

Help with carrying luggage to room

Lifts to upper floors

Access and facilities for disabled people

Internet availability

2. Desirable: things that it would be nice to have, e.g.:

In a restaurant

Some foods (appetisers) to eat before the meal, e.g. olives, nuts, flat bread, etc.

A mint chocolate or biscuit to go with a cup of coffee

A choice of cream, ice cream, yogurt or custard to go with their chosen dessert

A children's play area or table activities to occupy young children, e.g. colouring book and crayons

In a hotel

A range of toiletries (e.g. shampoo, shower gel, soap) in the bathroom of their room

A refrigerator to keep drinks, etc., cold

Air conditioning

Facilities to make hot drinks in the room

A hairdryer

A television or radio

3. Extras: things that customers do not expect or desire but are happy to be given:

In a restaurant

Vouchers for a free meal next time

A free bottle of wine with their meal

Free coffee refills at the end of the meal

In a hotel

Free transport to and from an airport or train station

Money-off vouchers for a future stay at the hotel

Free bottle of water, packet of sweets, nuts or biscuits

Accessible hotel bathroom for disabled customers

Customers want **consistent** (the same all the time) **good-quality** service from all parts of a H&C business, including:

- The **environment** of the business, which should be comfortable, warm, friendly and accessible to people with disabilities.

- The **ingredients** and **materials** used, which should include good-quality food, toilet and bathroom facilities, comfortable furniture and beds.

- The **opening hours** of the business, which suit a wide range of customers who want to eat, drink and socialise at different times of the day.

- The **customer service**, which should be provided by well-trained, helpful, polite, efficient and welcoming staff.

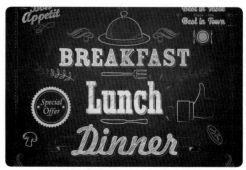

Providing good-quality customer service has many benefits:
- Customer satisfaction and loyalty
- More customers
- Staff feel more confident and happy
- Staff enjoy their job
- Fewer staff leave the job
- Fewer complaints from customers

Customer trends

Book link
pp61–62

There are more goods and services available than ever before, so businesses have a lot of competition and need to stay up to date in order to attract customers. The ways in which people choose and use H&C products and services include:

Self–service: e.g. buying food and drinks from a vending machine or drive-through food outlet

Online services: that are instant/fast/user-friendly/up to date with information technology (IT), e.g. for ordering takeaway meals to be delivered to their home

Social media/messaging (texts, emails, Twitter, Facebook, WhatsApp, etc.): for finding out and sharing information about H&C businesses, e.g. to comment on/review the products and services provided. Businesses also use these to attract and hold on to their customers.

Drive-through food outlet

Customers also expect:

- **Businesses to be available all the time**: e.g. to order takeaway food online for delivery at any time of day or night
- **A personalised service**: e.g. being able to find the type of restaurant they like, close to where they are, on their mobile phone
- **Dietary information**: e.g.:
  - Nutritional information about meals - available on menus and/or online
  - Food allergy and intolerance information to be shown clearly on the menu
  - Whether menu choices are suitable for particular dietary needs, e.g. vegetarian, vegan, dairy free, low salt, etc.
- **Environmentally sustainable and ethically conscious products and customer services**: businesses need to be aware of this for their customer service
- **Well-trained staff**: e.g. who understand dietary requirements and are able to answer customer questions about them

Food blogger using smartphone to write a review

Activity 6.1: Customer dietary requirements

Menus should show a range of dietary information so that customers are informed when they choose their food.

On the menu below, show where the following customer information (using the codes in the tables after the menu) should be printed, e.g.:

Wholewheat pasta with pesto and parmesan cheese:
Allergy advice: contains: G, N and L
Suitable for: V

Ordering food by smartphone

Menu

Starters

Wholewheat pasta with pesto and parmesan cheese

Spicy lentil and tomato soup, with flatbread

Garlic prawns with mayonnaise and salad

Main courses

Roasted vegetable tart with new potatoes and crisp green salad

Grilled chicken with peanut sauce, served with sweet potato wedges and peas

Cauliflower cheese with seasonal vegetables

Shepherd's pie with cheesy potato crust, sweetcorn and peas

<u>Desserts</u>

Panna cotta with fresh fruits

Rich chocolate mousse

Sticky toffee pudding with pecan fudge sauce

Lemon meringue pie

1. Allergy advice:

Key	Contains foods / ingredients known to cause allergies or intolerance
G	Gluten (wheat, barley, oats, rye)
N	Nuts / tree nuts / peanuts
C	Celery
F	Fish / shellfish / crustaceans (prawns, lobsters, etc.)
E	Eggs
L	Lactose (dairy foods – milk, cheese, cream, butter, yogurt)
S	Seeds (sesame, pumpkin, poppy, etc.)
B	Beans (soya beans, kidney beans, etc.)

2. Suitability:

Key	Suitable for
V	Suitable for vegetarians
VG	Suitable for vegans

The Hospitality and Catering industry is a major part of the leisure industry, which includes sports activities, holidays, tourism and outdoor activities (walking, water activities, etc.). The two areas work together very closely to provide customers with what they need, want and expect.

Book link pp63–64

Customer rights and equality

Book link p63

Customers are protected by various laws when they buy products or services. These include:

Trade Descriptions Act 1968

- Products and services must be described accurately and correctly

Equality Act 2010

- Protects the rights of individual people
- Protects people from unfair treatment
- Promotes equal opportunities for all people no matter what age, race, religion, gender they are or whether they have a disability

The Consumer Protection Act 1987

- It is against the law to sell unsafe products and services
- Health and safety information must be be given on products and services
- Correct prices must be given for products and services

Consumer Rights Act 2015

Products must:
- Be good quality
- Work correctly
- Match the description given about them
- Be fitted properly

Services must be:
- Carried out with care
- Completed for a reasonable price
- Completed within a reasonable time

Business and corporate needs and wants

Large businesses (corporates) and small businesses use the Hospitality and Catering industry for many types of events that they run, to provide a range of products and services:

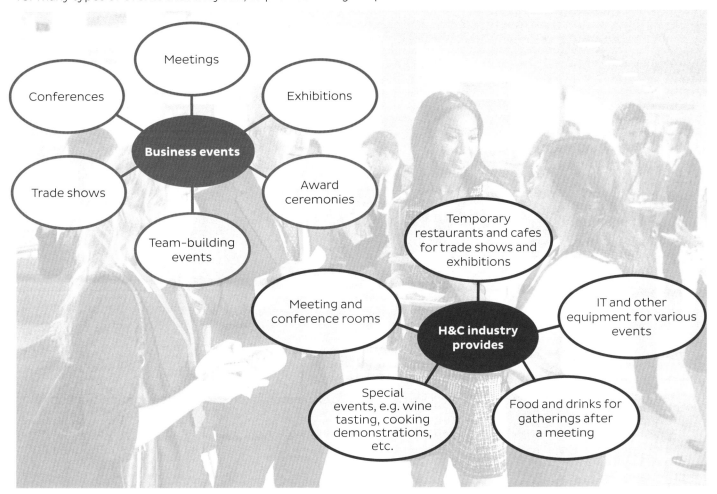

Local residents

If a H&C business is located in or near an area where people live, it should try to make sure that it meets the needs and expectations of local residents by:

- Employing local people
- Keeping noise from customers, music and cars to a low level, especially late in the evening
- Providing parking for customers to prevent traffic problems in local streets
- Employing security officers to maintain order and using CCTV cameras to monitor the local area
- Offering reasonable prices for hosting local events such as fetes, school proms and festivals

PLEASE LEAVE
QUIETLY
THIS IS A
RESIDENTIAL
AREA

Knowledge check – can you remember....?

1. The three levels for what customers need, want and expect, with an example for each in a restaurant or hotel?

2. Two good quality points for the environment of a H&C business?

3. Two good quality points for the ingredients and materials used in a H&C business?

4. Four benefits of good customer service?

5. Two trends in the ways in which customers choose and use products and services?

6. Three things that customers expect H&C businesses to provide with their products and services?

7. Two laws that protect customers when they buy products and services?

8. Three types of events that businesses and corporates run?

9. Three products and services that the Hospitality and Catering industry can provide for business events?

10. Two ways in which a H&C business can meet the needs and expectations of local residents?

E-assessment practice questions

Short answer questions

1. Customers have different needs, wants and expectations when they use a hospitality and catering business.

   List three essential needs that customers using a sports and leisure centre cafe would have. *[1 mark each]*

2. List three essential needs for customers with physical disabilities in a restaurant. *[1 mark each]*

Graduated lead-in questions

3. A new bar and restaurant has opened in a small town, and is situated in a residential area where there are lots of homes occupied by families with young children. The bar / restaurant will open seven days a week, from 2pm until 11pm, except on Sundays when it will open from 4pm until 10pm.
   a) Suggest two ways in which the managers of the bar / restaurant can prevent local residents from being disturbed at night and when customers leave *[2 marks]*
   b) Describe two ways in which the managers of the bar/restaurant could encourage local residents to become customers *[2 marks]*

4. The local town council in the town of Ashburness is going to host a ceremony at the Town Hall for local people who have each received an award for their work with local charities. The event will be sponsored by several large businesses, and there will be guests from a range of organisations invited to attend the ceremony.

   Suggest two products/services that a hospitality and catering business could provide at the event *[2 marks]*

Personal safety: responsibilities of employees and employers

Chapter 7

What do you need to know? (AC3.1)

- How to avoid accidents and injuries in the workplace

Book link
pp66–69

LO3 Understand how hospitality and catering provision meets health and safety requirements

Key learning

In the UK every year many employees have accidents or injuries while at work.

The main causes of accidents and injuries are:

- Slips, trips and falls
- Lifting/handling a heavy or awkward object
- Being hit by an object
- Being injured by a machine.

The Health and Safety Executive (HSE), is a government department that enforces health and safety rules and laws in the workplace.

The employers and all employees in H&C businesses are all responsible for personal safety in the workplace.

H&C businesses must make sure that they minimise the health and safety risks for their employees and customers.

 Remember!
An *employer* is someone who owns a business and pays an *employee* to work there.

Laws about personal safety

Health and Safety at Work Act (HASAWA)

What an employer must do by law	What an employee must do to follow the law and stay safe
<ul><li>Protect the health, safety and welfare of their employees and other people (e.g. customers, people making deliveries)</li><li>Minimise the risks that could cause injury or health problems in the workplace</li><li>Give information to employees about risks in the workplace and how they are protected</li><li>Give health and safety training to all employees</li></ul>	<ul><li>Take care of other people you work with who might be affected by what you do or do not do</li><li>Always follow the health and safety instructions your employer gives you</li><li>Go to health and safety training sessions</li><li>Use safety equipment properly</li><li>Report any safety or health hazards and problems with equipment, etc., to your employer</li></ul>

Reporting of Injuries, Diseases and Dangerous Occurrences Regulations (RIDDOR)

What an employer must do by law	What an employee must do to follow the law and stay safe
<ul><li>Report any serious workplace accidents, diseases and certain dangerous incidents (near misses) to the HSE</li></ul>	<ul><li>If you see or are worried about a health and safety problem, first tell the person in charge, your employer or your union representative</li><li>If nothing is done about it, you can report your worries to the HSE</li></ul>

Control of Substances Hazardous to Health Regulations (COSHH)

What an employer must do by law

- Make sure that employees are not exposed (without protection) to items and substances that are unsafe and /or harmful (hazardous) to their health
- These items and substances include:
  - Cleaning chemicals
  - Fumes, e.g. from machinery, cooking processes or vehicles
  - Dusts and powders e.g. icing sugar, flour, ground nuts
  - Vapours, e.g. from cleaning chemicals, machinery, pest control chemicals
  - Gases, e.g. from cookers
  - Biological agents e.g. pests and their waste products, moulds, bacteria
- Some of these substances can cause short- or long-term illnesses such as cancer, asthma, skin problems, liver damage

What an employee must do to follow the law and stay safe

- Go to training sessions
- Carefully follow the instructions for using hazardous substances
- Always wear safety equipment, e.g. gloves, masks, goggles, etc., that your employer gives you to use
- Make sure you learn the international symbols for different types of substances and how they can harm people:

Manual Handling Operations Regulations (MHOR)

What an employer must do by law

- Avoid risky manual handling operations if at all possible
- Assess any manual handling operations that cannot be avoided
- Reduce the risk of injury as far as possible, e.g. by using mechanical handling equipment such as fork-lift trucks
- Store heavy equipment, e.g. a food mixer, so that it is easy to take out and use; e.g. on a worktop or on a low shelf in a cupboard or storeroom

Manual handling means moving or supporting a load by lifting, putting down, pushing, carrying or moving it by hand or with the force of the body.

What an employee must do to follow the law and stay safe

- Go to training sessions on how to lift and handle loads
- Be aware of your own strengths and weaknesses
- 'Think before you lift'
- Do not take unnecessary risks
- Ask for help if you need it
- Check the load before you attempt to lift or move it – is it hot, cold, sharp, hard to grip, heavy, likely to be become unbalanced if it is moved?
- Check the area in which you are working – is there enough room to lift something properly? Is the flooring uneven, slippery, unstable? Are there steps or obstructions?
- Follow the advice on lifting heavy and large objects:
  - Squat down with your feet either side of the load to begin picking it up
  - Keep your back straight as you move to a standing position
  - Keep the load close to your body when you walk with it
  - Make sure you can see where you are going
  - Be very careful when lifting down heavy objects from high shelves. Use a purpose-built, sturdy set of step ladders or a step stool to stand on so that you can reach the object properly

wrong   right

Personal Protective Equipment (PPE) at Work Regulations (PPER)

What an employer must do by law

- Give employees PPE where it is needed
- Train employees so that they understand the importance of PPE
- Put up signs to remind employees to wear PPE
- Make sure that employees wear the PPE at all times when they are working in an area with health and safety risks
- Make sure PPE is good quality and is maintained properly

PPE protects different areas of the body, including:

- **Masks** to prevent breathing contaminated air into the lungs
- **Hard hats** and **reinforced shoes** to protect the head and feet from falling objects
- **Goggles/eye shields** to prevent the eyes being splashed with chemicals or injured by particles in the air

- **Thick/protective clothing** to prevent skin contact with heat, extreme cold or corrosive chemicals that burn the skin

What an employee must do to follow the law and stay safe

- Go to training sessions on the importance of and how to wear PPE
- Wear PPE as instructed by your employer, e.g.:
  - Chef's/cook's uniform to protect the body/arms from heat
  - Gloves and protective clothing when working in a freezer or handling frozen/chilled foods
  - Mask to protect the lungs when working with, e.g. flour, icing sugar, powdered nuts
  - Protective gloves for when using cleaning chemicals
  - Chain mail (metal) gloves or gauntlets (gloves with extensions that cover the arm up to the elbow) when using large sharp knives in butchery, e.g. boning and jointing a meat carcase
  - Reinforced and closed kitchen clogs or shoes to protect the feet from being injured by falling heavy objects or hot liquid spillage

Knowledge check – can you remember....?

1. Three main causes of accidents/injuries in the workplace?
2. Two things an *employer* must do under the Health and Safety at Work Act?
3. Two things an *employee* must do under the Health and Safety at Work Act?
4. Two things an *employer* must do under the Control of Substances Hazardous to Health Regulations?
5. Two things an *employee* must do under the Control of Substances Hazardous to Health Regulations?
6. Two things an *employer* must do under the Manual Handling Operations Regulations?
7. Two things an *employee* must do under the Manual Handling Operations Regulations?
8. Three types of Personal Protective Equipment used in the Hospitality and Catering industry?
9. Two things an *employer* must do under the Personal Protective Equipment at Work Regulations?
10. Two things an *employee* must do under the Personal Protective Equipment at Work Regulations?

Activity 7.1

Match the safety symbols used in the COSHH regulations to the correct type of harmful substance:

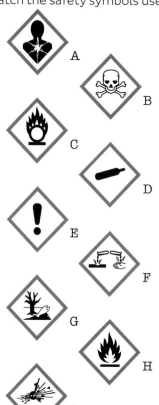

1 Substance that is dangerous for the environment

2 A gas under pressure that could explode

3 A substance that is corrosive (seriously damages the skin)

4 A substance that is toxic (poisonous)

5 A substance that causes long-term harm, e.g. cancer

6 A substance that is flammable (can catch fire)

7 A substance that can explode

8 A substance that should be used with caution

9 A substance that combines with oxygen in a chemical reaction

Activity 7.2

Match each of the following items of Personal Protective Equipment that should be worn with the correct activity that would take place in a catering kitchen:

Placing an item in the oven 1

Removing items from the freezer 2

Using cleaning chemicals 3

Cutting joints of meat 4

Working with icing sugar, flour or powdered nuts 5

Preparing food and walking to different places in the kitchen 6

Using oven cleaner spray 7

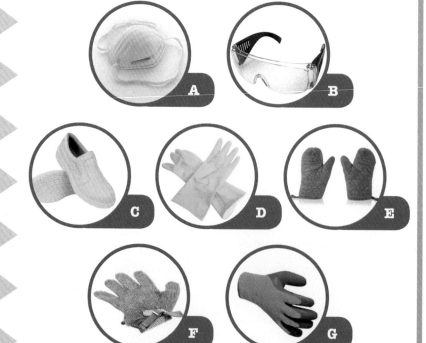

E-assessment practice questions

Short answer questions

1. In the UK every year many employees have accidents or injuries while at work.
   a) State two main causes of accidents and injuries in the workplace *[2 marks]*
   b) Identify the government department that enforces health and safety rules in the workplace *[1 mark]*
   c) List two additional types of accident/injury that could happen to a food handler working in a kitchen *[2 marks]*

2. The Personal Protective Equipment (PPE) at Work Regulations (PPER) require employers to train and provide their workforce with PPE to keep them safe.

   For each of the following workers in a large hotel, name one item of PPE that they should use: *[1 mark for each]*
   a) Chef in hotel kitchen
   b) Stock controller working in back of house
   c) Housekeeper cleaning bedrooms and bathrooms
   d) Gardener / grounds maintenance worker.

Stretch and challenge question

A new hotel is opening in a few weeks' time and has recruited staff for all the departments. Before the hotel opens for business, the management is running a training day on personal safety for all staff. The training will focus on the responsibilities that both the employers and employees have for personal safety.

Under each of the following laws, explain, giving reasons and examples, the responsibilities of both employers and employees for personal safety, i.e.:

- What an employer must do by law to make sure that the health and safety of their employees is protected
- What employees must do to make sure that they and the people they work with are safe.

a) Health and Safety at Work Act (HASAWA) *[6 marks]*

b) Control of Substances Hazardous to Health Regulations (COSHH) *[6 marks]*

c) Reporting of Injuries, Diseases and Dangerous Occurrences Regulations (RIDDOR). *[2 marks]*

Chapter 8

Book link
pp70–75

LO3 Understand how hospitality and catering provision meets health and safety requirements

Risks and control measures for personal safety in hospitality and catering

What do you need to know? AC3.2 AC3.3

- The difference between a *personal safety risk* and a *food safety risk*
- The types of personal safety risks that employees, employers, customers and suppliers may face in the Hospitality and Catering industry
- How personal safety risks can be controlled to prevent people's health being damaged or them being hurt
- How *security risks* can affect someone's safety and personal property

Key terms you should try to include in your answers

Control measure – an action or object used to reduce the risk of a hazard damaging a person's health or physically hurting them

Hazard – something that could damage a person's health or cause an accident that would physically hurt them

Personal safety risk – how likely it is that someone's health will be damaged or they will be hurt by a hazard

Risk assessment – a way of showing how much risk is involved in an activity, a situation or when using an object

Key learning

A **hazard** is something that could damage someone's health or cause an accident that would physically hurt (injure) them.

Here are two examples:

A health hazard – fine particles of flour dust that are produced when flour is sieved

A physical hazard – some food, water or oil spilt on the floor of a catering kitchen

A **personal safety risk** is how likely it is that someone's health will be damaged or they will be hurt by a hazard.

The personal safety risks for the two examples above are:

The flour dust particles that a baker breathes in when making bread every day for several years may gradually damage their lungs, and eventually the baker may not be able to breathe properly.

Food, water or oil spilt on the floor may cause a kitchen worker to slip, fall over and be physically hurt (injured).

Something that is **high risk** is more likely to damage someone's health or hurt them than something that is **low risk**.

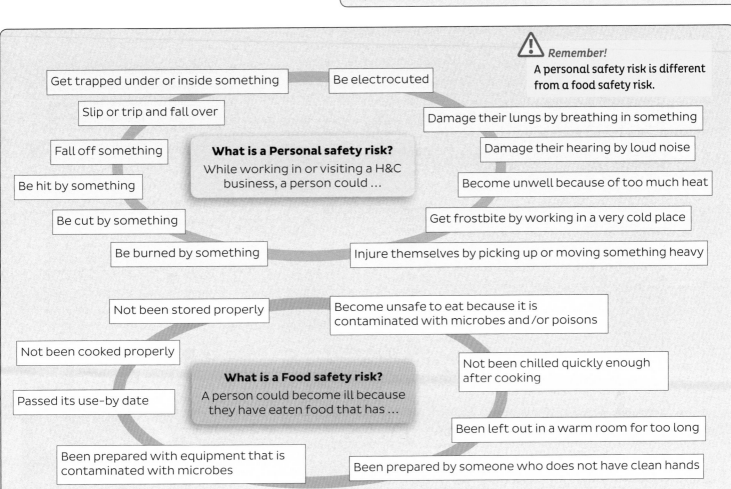

Get trapped under or inside something

Be electrocuted

⚠️ *Remember!*
A personal safety risk is different from a food safety risk.

Slip or trip and fall over

Damage their lungs by breathing in something

Fall off something

What is a Personal safety risk?
While working in or visiting a H&C business, a person could …

Damage their hearing by loud noise

Be hit by something

Become unwell because of too much heat

Be cut by something

Get frostbite by working in a very cold place

Be burned by something

Injure themselves by picking up or moving something heavy

Not been stored properly

Become unsafe to eat because it is contaminated with microbes and/or poisons

Not been cooked properly

What is a Food safety risk?
A person could become ill because they have eaten food that has …

Not been chilled quickly enough after cooking

Passed its use-by date

Been left out in a warm room for too long

Been prepared with equipment that is contaminated with microbes

Been prepared by someone who does not have clean hands

A **personal risk assessment** is used to show how much risk is involved in:

- An activity, e.g. carrying a heavy pan of hot food
- A situation, e.g. getting out of a building in an emergency
- Using an object, e.g. using a large slicing machine in the kitchen

A **control measure** is an action or object that is used to prevent or reduce the risk of a hazard damaging someone's health or hurting them.

The control measures for the two examples on page 54 are:

Example 1.

a) The baker should wear a mask to prevent breathing in the flour dust

b) Extractor fans should be used in the kitchen to remove dust particles from the air

Example 2.

a) Kitchen workers should wipe up spilt food, water or oil from the floor as soon as possible

b) Warning signs should be placed in an area where the floor is wet or slippery

55

The following charts give information about possible hazards and risks to the health, safety and security of people who work in or visit a H&C business, and the control measures used to control the risks:

⚠️ **Remember!**
An *employer* is someone who owns a business and pays an *employee* to work there.

Front of house employees:
Reception staff; Security staff; Waiting staff; Bar staff

Possible health hazards and risks	Control measures
• Muscle strain and back problems from lifting and carrying heavy items, moving tables and chairs, etc. Level of risk: medium to high	**Employers should:** • Give training on how to lift and carry heavy objects properly • Provide equipment, e.g. trolleys, to assist moving equipment and materials • Design customer service areas to limit the amount of twisting, reaching up, bending down and carrying that employees have to do
• Tiredness due to long working hours, leading to increased risk of injury Level of risk: medium to high	**Employers should:** • Limit the amount of repetitive work and standing for long periods of time that employees have to do • Provide them with sit-stand stools and anti-fatigue mats to stand on 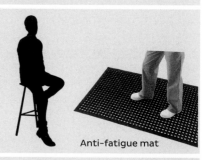 Anti-fatigue mat
• Stress: leading to high blood pressure, headaches, poor eating habits, days off sick from work, etc. – often caused by workload and problems between employees, e.g. bullying Level of risk: medium to high	**Employers should:** • Encourage good relationships between people in the workplace • Encourage employees to report work problems, and make changes where needed • Deal with workplace bullying and harassment when it is reported • Use counselling and support services for employees who are stressed

Possible safety risks	Control measures
• Slips, trip, falls • Burns and scalds from coffee machines, etc. • Electric shocks Level of risk: medium to high	**Employers should make sure that:** • All work areas are well lit, free from obstructions, and floors are in good condition • Equipment, e.g. ladders, is provided so employees can get items safely from high shelves, cupboards, etc. • Employees are trained to use all equipment correctly • Electrical wiring and equipment is safe to use and regularly tested • There are enough electrical safety switches and sockets so the wiring is not overloaded • Electrical equipment is kept away from water and wet areas • There are plenty of warning and safety signs to remind employees about safety • All emergency exits are working properly and do not have any obstructions that would stop people being able to get out in an emergency

Employees should:

- Wear non-slip shoes
- Wipe up any spills when they happen
- Make sure items are put away and drawers and doors are closed
- Avoid blocking passageways with boxes, equipment, etc.

Possible security risks AC3.2	Control measures AC3.3

- Physically and verbally aggressive customers
- Intruders coming into the building
- Personal belongings being stolen

Employers should:

- Employ security staff and enable other staff to contact them quickly from any part of the building
- Install closed-circuit television cameras (CCTV)
- Install security lighting outside the building, e.g. where bins are located near the back entrance to the kitchen
- Provide staff with security passes to go into the building and secure places to store their personal belongings when they are working

Employees should:

- Make sure they lock up their personal belongings in a secure place when working
- Report potential intruders to security staff

Back of house employees:
Chefs and cooks; Stock controller; Kitchen workers; Pot wash staff; Cleaners

Possible health hazards and risks AC3.2	Control measures AC3.3

Having contact with:

- Cleaning chemicals
- Extremes of heat and cold
- Diseases from pests

Possibly developing:

- Muscle and back strain from lifting, carrying and storing heavy items
- Muscle and back strain from:
  - bending awkwardly, e.g. cleaning the insides of large pots and ovens
  - reaching into a deep chest freezer
  - lifting heavy equipment or containers of ingredients
  - standing for a long time
- Repetitive strain injury, e.g. in the wrists and hands, from repeated chopping, kneading and mixing

Level of risk: medium to high

Employers should make sure that:

- Employees are given and wear protective equipment, e.g. rubber gloves, eye protection and masks, insulated gloves and clothing to work in cold areas
- Employees are trained to store and use chemicals safely and follow COSHH guidelines (see page 50)
- The kitchen is well ventilated and has air conditioning
- Employees always have water to drink when they are working
- The kitchen layout is designed so work stations are away from sources of heat
- Employees take plenty of rest breaks in a cool place
- Employees are trained how to lift and carry heavy objects correctly
- There is equipment, e.g. trolleys, plate dispensers, conveyors, etc., to help move heavy items and materials
- Staff can use machines for, e.g. mixing, kneading, cutting, slicing and peeling, to reduce strains to the hands and wrists

Air conditioning

57

- Workers have foot rails so they can move their bodyweight and reduce the stress to their back and legs
- If possible, workbenches of different heights are provided for food preparation, to avoid back strain when bending or reaching
- The kitchen and storerooms are regularly inspected and pest controlled

Possible safety risks **AC3.2**	Control measures **AC3.3**

Possible safety risks

- Slips, trip, falls
- Burns and scalds
- Cuts and scrapes
- Electric shocks

Level of risk: medium to high

Control measures

Employers should make sure that:

- All work areas are well lit, free from obstructions, and floors are in good condition
- Equipment, e.g. ladders, provided, so employees can get items safely from high shelves, cupboards, etc.
- All machinery has safety guards fitted
- Splatter guards are fitted around deep fat fryers to stop hot oil burns
- Guards are fitted around hot surfaces
- Hot liquids can be drained from large pans rather than being tipped out by hand
- Gas ovens, grills and hobs are regularly tested for, e.g., gas leaks and correct burning of the gas
- Electrical wiring and equipment is safe to use and regularly tested
- There are enough electrical safety switches and sockets so the wiring is not overloaded
- Electrical equipment is kept away from water and wet areas
- There are plenty of warning and safety signs to remind employees about safety
- Employees are trained to use all equipment correctly
- Employees are trained to give first aid in case of an injury
- All emergency exits are working properly and do not have any obstructions that would stop people being able to get out in an emergency

Employees should:

- Wear non-slip shoes
- Wear Personal Protective Equipment and clothing
- Wipe up any spills when they happen
- Remove any food that has fallen on the floor
- Make sure equipment is put away properly and drawers and doors are closed
- Avoid blocking passageways with boxes, equipment, etc.
- Carry and use knives safely
- Handle electrical equipment with dry hands
- Use oven cloths to handle hot baking trays and pan handles
- Report any safety problems to their manager/employer

Customers

Possible health hazards and risks **AC3.2**	Control measures **AC3.3**
• Food poisoning • Illness due to food allergies and intolerances Level of risk: low to medium	• Hazard Analysis of Critical Control Points (HACCP) – see Chapter 11 • Give customers information about ingredients in dishes on menus, so they can make safe choices

Possible safety risks **AC3.2**	Control measures **AC3.3**
• Trips, slips, falls • Fire or other emergency Level of risk: low to medium	**The managers of the business should make sure that:** • All customer areas are well lit, free from obstructions, floors are in good condition and steps/stairs are clearly marked and have handrails • All emergency exits are working properly and do not have any obstructions that would stop people being able to get out in an emergency

Possible security risks **AC3.2**	Control measures **AC3.3**
• Credit card fraud • Theft of personal belongings Level of risk: low to medium	**The managers of the business should make sure that:** • All customer payments are processed in front of the customer • Customers are provided with secure places to leave their belongings, e.g. a secure cloakroom, a digital safe in hotel bedrooms

Suppliers (who deliver to H&C businesses)

Possible health hazards and risks **AC3.2**	Control measures **AC3.3**
• Muscle strain and back problems from lifting, carrying and storing heavy items Level of risk: high to medium	**The managers of the business should make sure that:** • Employees are trained on how to lift and carry heavy objects properly • Equipment, e.g. trolleys, provided to help employees move equipment and materials safely

Possible safety risks **AC3.2**	Control measures **AC3.3**
• Trips, slips, falls • Fire or other emergency Level of risk: medium	**The managers of the business should make sure that:** • All areas are well lit, free from obstructions, floors are in good condition and steps/stairs are clearly marked and have handrails • All emergency exits are working properly and do not have any obstructions that would stop people being able to get out in an emergency

G CEREALS CONTAINING GLUTEN
CR CRUSTACEANS
E EGGS
F FISH
P PEANUTS
SO SOYBEANS
MI MILK (DAIRY)
N NUTS/ TREE NUTS
C CELERY
MU MUSTARD
S SESAME
SD SULPHUR DIOXIDE AND SULPHITES
L LUPIN
MO MOLLUSCS

Possible security risks AC3.2	Control measures AC3.3
• Attempted theft of property Level of risk: low	**The employees of the business should make sure that:** • They check the identity of callers to the business, e.g. suppliers • They lock away their personal belongings in a secure place

Activity 8.1

Every job has hazards and risks which need to be controlled. For each of the following groups of people who work in the H&C industry, find out, explain and describe why and how each piece of equipment is provided to help prevent damage to health, accidents and injuries at work, and risks to people's personal security.

Front of house employees: Reception staff; Security staff; Waiting staff; Bar staff

Equipment used to control health hazards and risks

Why and how do these pieces of equipment help to prevent health problems and accidents/injuries?

Trolley

Anti-fatigue mat

Sit-stand stool

Equipment or processes used to control personal safety hazards and risks

Why and how do these help to prevent accidents and injuries, and control emergencies?

Step ladder

Emergency escape route sign

PAT (Portable Appliance Testing) testing of electrical equipment

RCD (Residual Current Device) electrical safety unit in kitchen

Equipment or processes used to control personal security hazards and risks

Why and how do these help to prevent accidents and injuries, and control emergencies?

Security card to enter building

Staff lockers in rest room

CCTV camera in restaurant

Back of house employees: Chefs and cooks; Stock controller; Kitchen workers; Pot wash staff; Cleaners

Equipment/clothing used to control health hazards and risks

Why and how does this equipment/clothing help prevent health problems and accidents/injuries?

Working in the freezer warehouse of a food factory or stockroom

Extractor fans above a cooking range in a catering kitchen

Chilled water dispenser

Air conditioning unit outside on the roof of a catering kitchen

Large electric mixer

Equipment or processes used to control personal safety hazards and risks

Why and how do these help to prevent accidents and injuries, and control emergencies?

Blade guard

Warning sign

First aid kit

Temperature control and thermostat

Deep fat frying machine

Slicing Machine
Switch off/disconnect power supply at mains before cleaning. The guard provided must be in the correct position before operating the machine. Always return the slicing thickness indicator to the zero position when work is finished to avoid injury to hand.

Mopping up spilt liquid

Knife wallet

CAUTION WET FLOOR

Clean up all spillages immediately

Warning signs

Activity 8.2

Match each personal safety risk to the correct control measure used to prevent the health of someone being damaged or a person being hurt in a H&C business:

Personal safety risk

Carrying heavy boxes of wine from the delivery lorry to the bar	A
Having to lift a heavy food mixer from a high cupboard	B
Using electrical equipment in the kitchen	C
Storing and organising food in a walk-in freezer store room in a large hotel kitchen	D
Sieving large amounts of icing sugar every day for decorating cakes in a bakery	E
Using a knife to cut whole fresh chickens into separate pieces in a large hotel kitchen	F
Removing hot baking trays from the oven	G
Working in a very hot kitchen for 8 hours	H
Using a deep fat fryer to fry fish and chips	I
Reaching up for items of equipment and ingredients from high shelves	J

Which control measure?

1	Wear insulated clothes, gloves and shoes	
2	Ventilate the kitchen and drink plenty of water	
3	Safety test all electrical equipment	
4	Use a sack barrow	
5	Place a fire extinguisher and fire blanket near the frying area	
6	Use a stepladder	
7	Keep knives sharp so they work properly and safely	
8	Move heavy items to a worktop or low cupboard	
9	Use oven gloves	
10	Wear a mask	

Knowledge check – can you remember....?

1. What a hazard is?
2. What a personal safety risk is?
3. What a risk assessment is?
4. What a control measure is?
5. Two things an employer should do to prevent health hazards and risks in the front of house?
6. Two things an employee should do to prevent safety risks in the front of house?
7. Two things an employer should do to prevent security risks in the front of house?
8. Four things an employer should do to prevent health hazards and risks in the back of house?
9. Three things an employer should do to prevent safety risks in the back of house?
10. Four things an employee should do to prevent safety risks in the back of house?
11. Two things the managers of a business should do to prevent security risks for customers?
12. Two things employees should do to prevent security risks when suppliers deliver goods to the back of house?

E-assessment practice questions

Short answer questions

1. There are numerous personal safety risks that employees, employers, customers and suppliers may face in the Hospitality and Catering industry. List three personal safety risks. *[3 marks]*

2. A hazard is something that could damage a person's health or cause an accident that would physically hurt them. List three hazards that might be found in a catering kitchen. *[3 marks]*

Graduated lead-in question

3. In recent weeks, several front of house bar staff in a busy city bar and restaurant have been unable to work due to a number of health issues, including muscle strain and back problems, excessive tiredness and stress. The managers of the business are concerned and decide to investigate what control measures they can take to protect the health of their staff and enable all the staff to work without these health risks.

   a) Identify one reason for each of the following problems that have been reported by bar staff: *[3 marks]*

   Muscle strain and back problems

   Excessive tiredness

   Stress

   b) Suggest two control measures that the management could introduce to prevent each of these problems from happening in future: *[6 marks]*

   Muscle strain and back problems

   Excessive tiredness

   Stress

   c) Explain why it is important for the success of a hospitality and catering business to carry out risk assessments and put control measures in place for the personal safety and security of their front of house employees *[3 marks]*

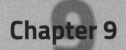

Chapter 9

Book link
pp76–85

LO4 Know how
food can cause ill
health

Food-related causes of ill health

What do you need to know?   AC4.1   AC4.4   AC4.5

- What makes food become unsafe to eat and makes people ill
- How to prevent people being ill because of something they have eaten
- How and why all food handlers must be trained to keep food safe to eat

Key learning

There are three main causes of food-related ill health:

1. Microbes
2. Chemicals, metals and poisonous plants
3. Food allergies and intolerances (see pages 71–74)

Key terms you should try to include in your answers

Bacteria – tiny living things, some of which cause food poisoning

Contaminate – make a food unsafe to eat by infecting it with microbes that will grow and multiply in it

Cross-contamination – how microbes are spread from one place onto some food

Microbes – tiny plants and animals that you can only see under a microscope (also called micro-organisms)

Moulds – tiny plants, similar to mushrooms

Pathogenic – something that makes people ill

Toxins – another name for poisons; if something is toxic, it is poisonous

Microbes

Book link
pp76–78

You need to be able to explain:	What you need to know about microbes
What microbes are	They are: ● Tiny plants and animals ● Often called micro-organisms ● So small, you can only see them clearly under a microscope.
What microbes are called	There are three groups: ● **Bacteria** ● **Moulds** ● Yeasts There are many different types of each.
Where microbes come from	● They are found in many places: air, water, soil, dust, dirt, sewage, food, food packaging, clothes, rubbish, surfaces, equipment, people, insects, animals, birds ● They are so small that it is usually impossible to know they are there.
What microbes do to food	● They live on or in food, where they grow and multiply ● They make the food unsafe to eat, and often smell, taste and look bad ● If food is stored, handled, prepared and cooked properly, it is possible to slow down or prevent microbes from growing and multiplying in it.
What makes microbes grow and multiply	● The right temperature ● Water (moisture) ● Food to eat ● Time to grow ● The right amount of acid or alkali (pH) ● In the right conditions, bacteria can multiply every 15 minutes.

Why microbes make food unsafe and unfit to eat	• They put **waste products** and poisons into the food
	• If people eat these, they become ill with **food poisoning**
	• Large numbers of microbes in a food can make people ill because they irritate the digestive system
	• Not all microbes make people ill
	• Some microbes are needed for food production, e.g.:
	  – some types of bacteria are used to make yogurt
	  – yeast is used to make bread
	  – some moulds are used to make cheeses, e.g. Brie, Blue Stilton
	• Microbes that do make people ill are called **pathogenic** (harmful) **microbes**.

What food handlers can do to stop microbes making food unsafe	• **Prevent cross-contamination** by:
	  – **washing their hands** before handling food; after handling raw meat, poultry, fish and eggs; after visiting the toilet; after putting food waste in the bin, after sneezing into a tissue
	  – **keeping raw and cooked foods separate** during storage and using separate equipment to prepare them
	  – **using colour-coded boards and knives** to prepare different types of food
	• **Cook** food to a high temperature (at least 70°C) which will kill many microbes
	• **Cool** food to a low temperature (0–5°C in a refrigerator). Microbes will still grow and multiply, but only very slowly
	• **Freeze** food (minus 18°C to minus 22°C in a freezer). Microbes will become inactive (dormant) **but will still be alive**
	• **Dry** food by taking out moisture, which will kill many microbes
	• **Cover** food and store it correctly to stop microbes getting into it
	• **Preserve** food by killing microbes:
	  – in acid (e.g. vinegar in pickles)
	  – in salt (e.g. dried salted fish)
	  – in sugar (e.g. jam).

Food poisoning AC4.1 AC4.4 AC4.5

 Book link p77

What is food poisoning?	What are the signs (symptoms) that someone has food poisoning?		Notes

• A common and nasty illness that can lead to serious health problems
• Harmful (pathogenic) bacteria are the main cause of food poisoning
	Signs you cannot see
	Headache
	Weakness
	Feeling cold and shivery
	Bad stomach ache
	Feeling sick
	Do not want to eat food
	Aching muscles
		Signs you can see
		Diarrhoea
		High body temperature
		Being sick (vomiting)
		Dizziness
			• A person with food poisoning is not likely to have all these signs
			• Different types of bacteria cause different symptoms
			• A person can start to feel ill after a few hours to several days after they have eaten **contaminated** food
			• They may feel ill for several days
			• Food poisoning is very dangerous for:
			  – young children
			  – pregnant women
			  – elderly people
			  – people who have been ill
			  – people who have a weak immune system

Bacteria

Book link
pp79–80

This chart will help you remember the most common food poisoning bacteria:

Bacteria name	Which foods it is usually found in	Signs of food poisoning	How long it takes for this bacteria to make someone ill
Bacillus cereus			1–16 hours
Campylobacter	Not heat treated Dirty water		48–60 hours
E. coli (Escherichia coli)	Not heat treated Dirty water	+ kidney damage	12–24 hours
Salmonella			12–36 hours
Listeria	Made from untreated milk Unwashed salad Pâté	Feels like having the flu\n\nCan cause miscarriage of unborn baby	1–70 days
S. aureus (Staphylococcus aureus)	Not heat treated\n\nHands Runny nose Wound/cut		1–6 hours

What happens to bacteria at different temperatures?

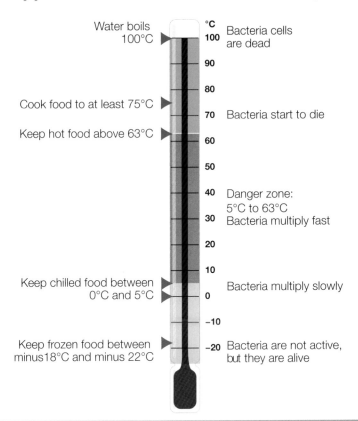

Water boils 100°C ► 100 — Bacteria cells are dead

90

80

Cook food to at least 75°C ► 70 — Bacteria start to die

Keep hot food above 63°C ► 60

50

40 — Danger zone: 5°C to 63°C

30 — Bacteria multiply fast

20

10

Keep chilled food between 0°C and 5°C ► 0 — Bacteria multiply slowly

−10

Keep frozen food between minus18°C and minus 22°C ► −20 — Bacteria are not active, but they are alive

Activity 9.1: Which food poisoning bacteria are found in which foods and liquids?

Look at the pictures of different foods and liquids.

Match which types of food poisoning bacteria are found in the different foods and liquids.

Remember that more than one type of bacteria may be found in a food or liquid.

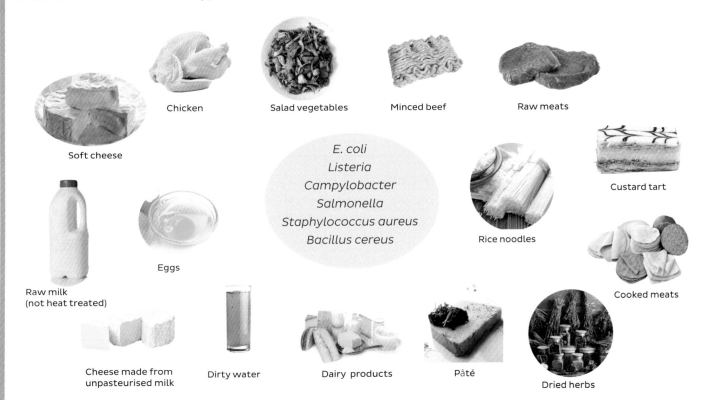

Soft cheese

Chicken

Salad vegetables

Minced beef

Raw meats

E. coli
Listeria
Campylobacter
Salmonella
Staphylococcus aureus
Bacillus cereus

Custard tart

Rice noodles

Eggs

Cooked meats

Raw milk (not heat treated)

Cheese made from unpasteurised milk

Dirty water

Dairy products

Pâté

Dried herbs

Activity 9.2: Storing foods

Look at the images of the foods in the table below.

For each food, choose the best way of storing it from column A, and the reason why you would store it this way from column B (the first one has been done for you as an example):

A How would you store it?		B Why would you store it this way?	
1	In a refrigerator	A	It is a low-risk food that does not need to be chilled
2	In a well-ventilated cupboard or room (not in a kitchen)	B	It is a high-risk food so must be chilled to slow microbial growth
3	In a kitchen cupboard	C	It is a high-risk food because it has been opened and must be chilled
4	In an airtight container	D	It is likely to go stale and soft because it will pick up moisture from the air
5	In a dark, cool place	E	It may be contaminated by insects if it is left uncovered
6	Uncovered in a kitchen or other room	F	It is likely to react to light and become a health risk
		G	It needs time to ripen
		H	It will lose water and wilt if left in a warm place

Food		How would you store it?	Why would you store it this way?
	A raw chicken	1	B
	1. A can of baked beans		
	2. An opened carton of long-life milk		
	3. An opened packet of flour		
	4. Shortbread		
	5. Raw potatoes		
	6. A hard mango		
	7. A lettuce		
	8. A pack of fresh minced beef		
	9. Left-over meat curry		
	10. An iced fruit birthday cake		

Moulds

Moulds make food unsafe and unfit to eat by:

- Sending out tiny spores ('seeds') which land on the surface of food
- The spores **germinate** (start to grow) and send down roots into the food if conditions are right
- You can see large numbers of moulds growing on food
- Moulds make food taste and smell very unpleasant
- The waste products produced by the mould go into the food through the roots
- The waste products contain poisons (**toxins**) that can make people ill
- The waste products can stay in the food even if the mould you can see is cut off.

Yeasts

Yeasts are found in the air. They make food unsafe and unfit to eat by:

- Settling on food and breaking down (**fermenting**) any sugars it contains into **CO_2 gas** and alcohol
- You can see yeasts growing on food, as they produce small brown spots on the surface
- Foods such as fruit yogurts, dried fruit and fruit juices can be spoiled by yeasts
- Wild yeasts are used to make sourdough bread, which is safe to eat

Apple with yeasts growing on the skin

Chemicals, metals and poisonous plants

Chemicals

Sometimes food becomes contaminated with chemicals that are poisonous and will make people ill very soon after they have entered their body. Some other chemicals gradually build up in the body over many months or years, and may eventually cause illnesses such as cancer, liver and kidney failure. Chemicals may get into food because of **environmental pollution**, e.g. from factories that let chemicals get into rivers and the sea or soil.

To avoid food being contaminated with chemicals in the food industry:

- Food handlers **must not**:
  - Accidentally add too much of a food additive, e.g. food colourings or preservatives, to food products when they are being made
  - Use too much of a cleaning product when cleaning equipment in a food factory or catering kitchen
  - Store a chemical, e.g. bleach, in an unlabelled container, as it may be added by mistake to a food.
- Farmers **must not**:
  - Use too much of a chemical pesticide or fertiliser on plant foods that are being grown.

Metals

Some metals are poisonous if they get into the body, e.g. aluminium, copper, lead, iron, tin, zinc. Some old cooking pans, which were made from aluminium, copper, zinc or iron would react with acids in foods such as lemons, rhubarb, tomatoes and wine and the metal would get into the food. Pans made from stainless steel do not react with acids.

Poisonous plants

Some plants contain natural substances that are poisonous to humans, e.g.:

- Raw red kidney beans. These contain a poison and must be boiled for at least 15 minutes to destroy it. Canned red kidney beans have already been cooked and are safe to eat.

- Mouldy nuts and cereals, e.g. corn.
  The mould produces a poisonous substance.

- Rhubarb leaves contain a poisonous acid.
  The stems are safe to eat.

- Poisonous wild mushrooms.
  Many wild mushrooms are poisonous.
  The picture shows the 'death cap' mushroom, which is one the most poisonous fungi known to exist. If eaten, the poison it contains quickly damages the liver and other organs in the body. It has caused many deaths.

Knowledge check – can you remember....?

1. What a microbe is?
2. Two types of microbes?
3. Four places where microbes are found?
4. Three things that microbes need to grow and multiply?
5. Why microbes make food unsafe and unfit to eat?
6. Two ways that food handlers can prevent the cross-contamination of microbes into food?
7. What happens to microbes when food is frozen?
8. What happens to microbes when food is stored in a refrigerator?
9. Three signs (symptoms) of food poisoning that you cannot see?
10. Two signs (symptoms) of food poisoning that you can see?
11. Two groups of people for whom food poisoning is very dangerous?
12. The names of two bacteria that cause food poisoning?
13. Two foods where Salmonella is often found?
14. How moulds start to grow on foods?
15. What bacteria do in the temperature Danger Zone?
16. Why stainless-steel pans are used in food preparation?
17. Why food should be cooked to at least 70°C?
18. Why cleaning chemicals must not be stored near foods in unlabelled containers?

E-assessment practice questions

Short answer questions

1. List two main causes of food-related illness *[2 marks]*

2. State two reasons why microbes make food unfit to eat *[2 marks]*

3. Suggest three ways in which food handlers can stop microbes making food unsafe *[3 marks]*

4. Explain why the following practices are important:
   a) Keeping hot chicken curry above 63°C in serving dishes at a buffet *[1 mark]*
   b) Keeping fresh cream cakes at 0°C to 5°C in a bakery shop *[1 mark]*

Food allergies and intolerances

Chapter 10

What do you need to know? AC4.1 AC4.5

- What a food allergy and a food intolerance are
- How food allergies and intolerances affect people's health
- Which foods cause food allergies and intolerances

Book link
pp86–91

LO4 Know how food can cause ill health

Key learning

Food handlers need to know about what causes people to have a **food allergy** or **intolerance** so they can:

- Avoid contaminating foods with food allergens (ingredients that people are allergic to) when preparing food
- Tell customers about the ingredients in the food they are selling or serving them
- Make sure that menus show all the ingredients they contain, so that customers avoid buying foods they know they cannot eat
- Recognise and know what to do if a customer becomes ill with a food allergy.

Key terms you should try to include in your answers

Allergen – something that causes an allergy

Anaphylaxis – a very severe and life-threatening allergic reaction that affects breathing, the heart, the digestive system and the skin

Food allergy – a condition where the body's immune system reacts to certain foods, which causes a range of symptoms

Food intolerance – a long-term health condition where certain foods make someone unwell

Food allergy AC4.1 AC4.5

Book link
pp86–88

What is a food allergy?	What are the signs (symptoms) that someone has a food allergy?		Notes

• A food allergy is a serious and possibly life-threatening reaction to certain foods
• It is caused by the body reacting to something in the food (an **allergen**)
• A severe allergic reaction is called **anaphylaxis**, which can cause death – the person must have medical treatment immediately
• Someone who is allergic to foods must:
  – avoid eating them
  – read food labels carefully to see if those foods are in the ingredients list (food allergens are shown in bold lettering on food labels)
	Signs that happen inside the body that you cannot see
	• The mouth, tongue and throat swell
	• The person cannot breathe, speak or swallow properly
	• Wheezing
	• Stomach pain
	• Feeling sick – may be sick
	• Blood pressure drops
	• They may collapse and become unconscious
		Signs you can see
		• Skin becomes red
		• A raised, red/pink itchy rash shows on the skin (called hives)
		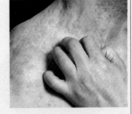
		• The skin swells – often on the face
		• The nose and eyes itch
		• The lips and eyelids swell
		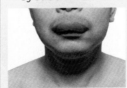
			An allergic reaction can happen within a few seconds, minutes or hours after eating the food.
			
			If someone has an allergic reaction:
			• Stay calm and call 999 for an ambulance
			• Make the patient comfortable
			• If they have an EpiPen, use it (it will control their symptoms while they are going to hospital)
			• People who work for a H&C business should be trained to use an EpiPen

an EpiPen

The most common foods that cause allergies are:

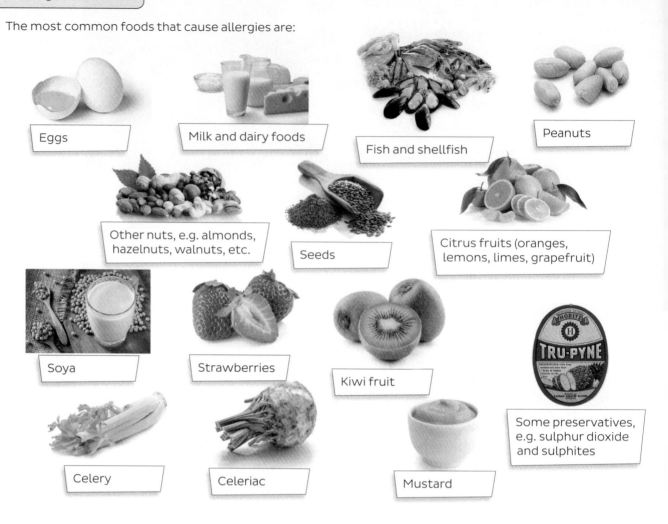

Eggs

Milk and dairy foods

Fish and shellfish

Peanuts

Other nuts, e.g. almonds, hazelnuts, walnuts, etc.

Seeds

Citrus fruits (oranges, lemons, limes, grapefruit)

Soya

Strawberries

Kiwi fruit

Celery

Celeriac

Mustard

Some preservatives, e.g. sulphur dioxide and sulphites

Food intolerance AC4.1 AC4.5

Book link pp89–91

Food intolerance happens when something in certain foods makes someone feel unwell most of the time but is not as life-threatening as a food allergy can be. People with a food intolerance may have a range of symptoms:

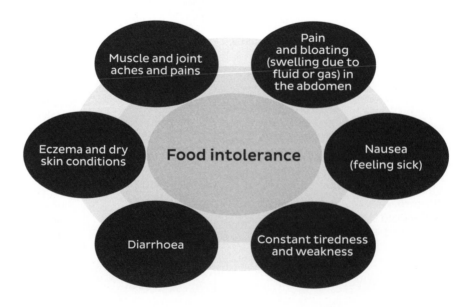

Muscle and joint aches and pains

Pain and bloating (swelling due to fluid or gas) in the abdomen

Eczema and dry skin conditions

Food intolerance

Nausea (feeling sick)

Diarrhoea

Constant tiredness and weakness

Lactose intolerance

Lactose is the natural sugar found in dairy milk (from cows, goats, sheep etc.). People who have lactose intolerance cannot digest (break down and absorb) lactose in their body, so the bacteria in their large intestine break it down instead. This produces a lot of gas and causes bloating (swelling) of the abdomen (belly/tummy), flatulence (wind/gas), abdominal (belly/tummy) pain, diarrhoea and nausea (feeling sick). People with lactose intolerance must not eat dairy foods or foods that contain them.

Lactose/dairy- free food products

Which foods contain lactose?

All dairy foods (milk, cheese, yogurt, cream, butter, crème fraiche, sour cream, cream cheese, whey and milk powder), and any foods that contain them (e.g. cakes, biscuits, desserts, some snack foods and sweets, some ready meals, sauces, custard, chocolate, some vegetable fat spreads, ice cream etc.) contain lactose.

 Remember!
Eggs are not a dairy food and do not contain lactose.

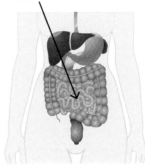

It is possible to buy lactose-free or dairy-free food products such as milks and yogurts.

Coeliac disease

Coeliac disease is a condition that involves the body's immune system, but it is not an allergy. Someone who has this condition is called a coeliac.

The small intestine in the body is lined with thousands of tiny finger-like projections called villi. Normally, the villi allow lots of nutrients from the food we eat to be absorbed and then sent into the bloodstream to go round the body.

Coeliac disease is caused by the immune system not tolerating gluten, which is found in wheat, barley, oats and rye and food products that contain them. This causes the villi in the small intestine to become damaged, so they cannot absorb enough nutrients into the body:

The small intestine

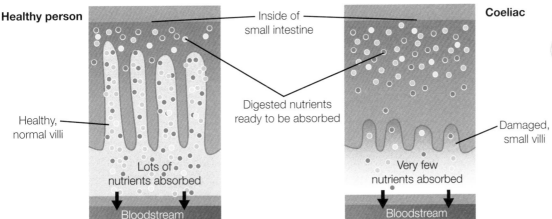

If someone has coeliac disease:

- They will not have enough nutrients going into their body
- They will not have enough energy and will be tired much of the time
- They can lose weight and become ill
- Children with coeliac disease might not grow properly.

Coeliacs must not eat any food containing gluten. This will allow the villi in their small intestine to gradually get better and work properly.

Which foods contain gluten?

Gluten is found in wheat, barley, oats and rye and food products that contain them, e.g. pasta, bread, pizza, cakes, pies, pastries, buns, croissants, biscuits, snack bars, crackers, seasonings and spice mixes, breakfast cereals, sausages, burgers and other processed meats, couscous, semolina, soy sauce, noodles, malt vinegar, some beers and ales.

It is possible to buy gluten-free food products in most supermarkets.
They often show a gluten free symbol, like this one:

Activity 10.1

Look at the lunch menu choices below for patients in a hospital:

Getwell Hospital

Lunch menu

Choose 1 item from each group:

A.

Cream of chicken soup with bread roll

Mixed leaf and avocado salad with olive oil dressing

Vegan lentil pâté with wheat crackers

*

B.

Roasted vegetable and pasta in cheese sauce

Baked chicken breast, stuffed with mozzarella cheese and herbs, served with seasonal vegetables

Vegan chickpea and coconut curry

*

C.

Fresh fruit salad

Chocolate mousse, served with a shortbread biscuit

Traditional apple crumble and custard

*

---

1. Describe and explain how the chefs could change the ingredients in some of the menu choices to suit a patient who has lactose intolerance.

2. Describe and explain how the chefs could change the ingredients in some of the menu choices to suit a patient who has coeliac disease.

Knowledge check – can you remember….?

1. What a food allergy is?

2. What food intolerance is?

3. Two things that a food handler should do to help people who have food allergies or intolerances?

4. Three visible signs (symptoms) that someone is having an allergic reaction to food?

5. Five of the most common foods that cause allergies?

6. Three visible or non-visible signs (symptoms) that someone has a food intolerance?

7. Two signs (symptoms) that someone has lactose intolerance?

8. Two foods someone with lactose intolerance should not eat?

9. Two foods that someone with coeliac disease should not eat?

10. Two visible or non-visible signs (symptoms) that someone has coeliac disease?

E-assessment practice questions

Short answer questions

1. Suggest one way in which a waiter in a restaurant can help a customer who has food allergies to choose from the menu *[1 mark]*

2. How are food allergens shown on a food label? *[1 mark]*

3. List three foods that someone who has lactose intolerance cannot eat *[3 marks]*

4. List three foods that people with coeliac disease cannot eat *[3 marks]*

Stretch and challenge question

A catering company has been asked to prepare a cold buffet lunch for a group of twenty people on a training course. Four of the people have coeliac disease.

Plan a menu for:
- Four savoury main course dishes, plus three side dishes /accompaniments
- Two desserts, plus two accompaniments.

The menu must include some dishes that the coeliacs will be able to eat.

Explain which dishes are suitable for the coeliacs and why.

Explain how the catering company will enable the coeliacs to identify and choose the dishes that are suitable for them to eat.

Chapter 11

Food safety legislation

What do you need to know? **AC4.3**

- How the law protects people who buy food (consumers) from food poisoning
- How the law makes sure that there are high standards of food safety in the food industry

Book link
pp92–99

LO4 Know how food can cause ill health

Key learning

Many people are affected by food poisoning each year.

Food poisoning can be prevented.

Food safety laws make sure that food is safe to eat.

Food safety laws

Book link
pp92–93

Food safety laws protect:

Consumers	Food businesses
• To stop them getting food poisoning • To make sure all food businesses have high food safety standards • To take action if a food business breaks the law	• To make sure all food handlers are trained in food safety • To make sure working conditions are good so food handlers can obey the law • To prevent consumers making false claims about being ill after eating some food

All parts of the food industry are covered by food safety laws, including:

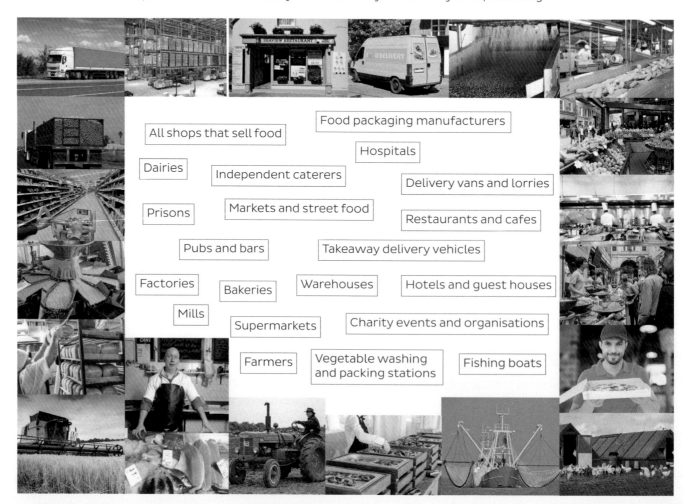

All shops that sell food

Food packaging manufacturers

Hospitals

Dairies

Independent caterers

Delivery vans and lorries

Prisons

Markets and street food

Restaurants and cafes

Pubs and bars

Takeaway delivery vehicles

Factories

Bakeries

Warehouses

Hotels and guest houses

Mills

Supermarkets

Charity events and organisations

Farmers

Vegetable washing and packing stations

Fishing boats

All laws are complicated. You are not expected to know all the details of food safety laws, but you need to understand the basic **rules** and the **responsibilities** of people who work in a H&C business to make sure the laws are followed. These are set out on the following pages.

1. The Food Safety Act 1990

Book link
p94

All food businesses must make sure that all the food they produce for sale or give away is:

1. Safe to eat
2. What people expect it to be
3. Not labelled, advertised or presented in a way that is confusing or not true

2. Food Hygiene Regulations (rules)

Book link
pp94–98

Anyone who owns, manages or works in a food business, whatever its size, must:

1. Make sure food is handled, supplied and sold in a hygienic way.
2. Identify possible **food safety hazards** in all the operations and activities of the food business.
3. Know which stages in their food-handling activities are critical for food safety: i.e. the stages at which things could go wrong – the **critical control points**.
4. Decide what **controls** can be put in place to prevent risks to food safety.
5. Make sure that food safety controls are in place, are always followed by everyone and are regularly maintained and reviewed.

The Food Hygiene Regulations cover:

HACCP

Book link
pp94–96

All food businesses must:

- Protect the health of their customers
- Show **due diligence** in the operation and activities of their business: this means they have carried out reasonable actions to avoid a food safety risk

To make sure all the things that the Food Hygiene Regulations (rules) require are done properly, a food safety management system called **Hazard Analysis of Critical Control Points (HACCP)** is used.

> **HACCP –Hazard Analysis of Critical Control Points**

| What are the **critical control points**? Each stage of food production | *Analysis* What are the **hazards** at each stage? | *Analysis* How are these hazards **controlled**? | *Analysis* How are the controls **checked** |

The word 'analysis' means that the operation of the food business is separated into stages. Each stage is looked at in detail to identify possible hazards and explain how these are controlled to prevent a food safety risk.

A food business should produce evidence that they have carried out a HACCP, so that an Environmental Health Officer (see pages 85–86) can check it when they carry out an inspection.

To help you understand what HACCP means, on the next page is a detailed example of a HACCP document for a cafe that sells hot and cold lunches, as well as hot and cold drinks. The critical control points, hazards, controls and correct temperatures used to prevent food safety risks are all clearly set out.

Key terms you should try to include in your answers

Critical control points – stages in a food-production operation where food safety could go wrong

Due diligence – being able to prove that reasonable actions have been taken to avoid a health risk

Hazard Analysis of Critical Control Points (HACCP) – a food safety management system to identify possible hazards to food safety

Stage of food production: Critical control points	Possible hazards	Controls and checks used to prevent a food safety risk	What are the correct temperatures?
Buying the food	• Chilled or frozen foods delivered to cafes might not be cold enough, so bacteria could multiply	• Food suppliers are visited regularly to check what HACCP controls they have in place • Temperature (and cleanliness) of chilled delivery van/lorry is checked at each delivery, before accepting the foods	• The temperature of delivery van/lorry must be: **0°C to 5°C for chilled foods** **minus 18°C to minus 22°C for frozen foods**
Storing the food	• Bacteria may grow and multiply in chilled and frozen foods if they are not stored at the right temperatures	• Refrigerator and freezer temperatures are checked every day and recorded in a log book • Refrigerator and freezer motors and door seals are regularly checked and serviced to make sure they work properly • Alarms that make a warning noise if the inside temperature goes up too much are fitted to the refrigerators and freezers to warn the kitchen staff • The dates on all stored foods are regularly checked and older foods are used up first (FIFO – first in, first out)	Refrigerators: **0°C to 5°C** (**up to 8°C** in Wales and Scotland) Freezers: **minus 18°C to minus 22°C**
	• Dry foods will go mouldy if they become damp	• Dry foods are stored in a ventilated room, on shelves in airtight containers	
	• Bacteria could spread from one food to another	• Raw and cooked foods are kept separate in the refrigerators to prevent cross-contamination	
	• Pests can contaminate food and make it unsafe to eat	• Pest traps are placed inside the storage area • Regular pest control inspections are carried out • Loose foods are stored in pest-proof containers	
Preparing the food	• Bacteria could spread from one food to another	• Colour-coded chopping boards and knives are used for different foods • Raw foods are prepared in a separate area from cooked foods • Frozen high-risk foods (meat, poultry, fish, cream) are defrosted on a tray in the refrigerator	Defrost foods at: **0°C to 5°C**

	• Bacteria from the soil could contaminate food • Food handlers could contaminate food with bacteria from their hands, body or clothes	• All vegetables and fruits are washed before storage and preparation • All staff have passed their Food Safety and Hygiene training and have up-to-date certificates • All staff wear clean uniform each day	
Cooking the food	• High-risk foods such as meat, poultry, fish and seafood may not be cooked all the way through, so harmful bacteria could still be alive	• Food probes are used to measure the temperature at the core (centre) of the cooked food before serving to customers	Core temperature: **minimum 70°C for 2 minutes**
Cooling cooked food for storage	• Bacteria could multiply in cooked food if it is not cooled quickly enough before being stored in the refrigerator or freezer	• Cooked rice is rapidly cooled in cold water and then refrigerated • Other cooked dishes are covered and cooled in a ventilated room away from the kitchen before being refrigerated or frozen	Cooked foods should reach: **5°C or lower within 1½ hours**
Reheating cooked and chilled foods	• Bacteria can multiply in reheated foods if they are not heated right through	• Food probes are used to measure the temperature at the core (centre) of the reheated food before serving to customers • Foods are reheated only once	Minimum core temperature: **70°C for 2 minutes** in England, Wales and Northern Ireland. In Scotland the core temperature must be: **minimum of 82°C**
Keeping the food hot or cold before serving to customers	• Bacteria may multiply inside cooked meat, poultry or fish and seafood dishes if they are not kept hot enough before serving	• Food probes are used to measure the temperature at the core (centre) of the hot food before serving to customers	Core temperature: **minimum 63°C**
	• Bacteria can multiply in chilled foods, e.g. salads, cooked cold meats, pâtés, cold desserts containing eggs and cream, if they are not kept cold enough	• All high-risk cold desserts, salads, cooked cold meats, pâtés, cream etc. are refrigerated until served to customers	**0°C to 5°C**
Washing up and cleaning	• Bacteria will multiply on pieces of food if they are left on equipment, plates, dishes and cutlery	• All equipment, plates, dishes, cups, glasses and cutlery are washed in a dishwashing machine and air dried in an area away from contamination	Hand washing: **55°C** with washing up liquid Rinse in very hot water: **82°C** Dishwashers: **82°C to 89°C**

Getting rid of food waste and rubbish	• Bacteria and moulds will multiply in food waste and rubbish • Microbes will live and multiply on the lids and inside waste bins	• Waste bins are located outside the kitchen • Waste bins are foot operated so staff do not need to touch the lids • Waste bins are collected and emptied regularly • Staff are trained to wash their hands after handling food waste and rubbish
Cleaning the kitchen	• Microbes will multiply on all surfaces, in corners, on ceilings, under kitchen units etc. • Sink units and drains are ideal places for bacteria to grow and multiply	• The kitchen surfaces, walls, floors and sinks are washed and dried at the end of every working day using cleaning chemicals • Twice a week the refrigerator shelves are cleared and cleaned • Twice a year the extractor hoods in the kitchen are taken down and cleaned • Twice a year, the kitchen has a deep clean

Food premises (buildings, rooms, washrooms, etc.) where food is prepared

Book link
p96

These premises:

Must be

Clean and well maintained

Hygienic

Easy to keep clean

Free from pests

Well lit

Well ventilated

Must have

A supply of safe drinking water

Enough space for people to work in

Good drainage to get rid of dirty water

Good, hygienic staff washing and toilet facilities

A good waste disposal system

Responsibilities of food handlers

Book link
p97

They must have good personal hygiene:

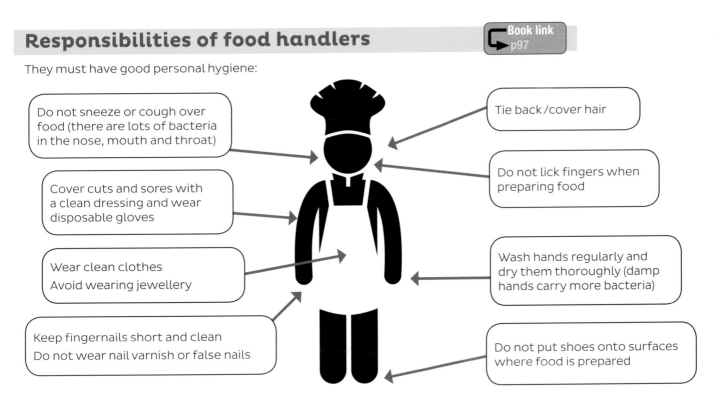

Do not sneeze or cough over food (there are lots of bacteria in the nose, mouth and throat)

Tie back / cover hair

Do not lick fingers when preparing food

Cover cuts and sores with a clean dressing and wear disposable gloves

Wear clean clothes
Avoid wearing jewellery

Wash hands regularly and dry them thoroughly (damp hands carry more bacteria)

Keep fingernails short and clean
Do not wear nail varnish or false nails

Do not put shoes onto surfaces where food is prepared

They must **prevent cross-contamination** of bacteria:

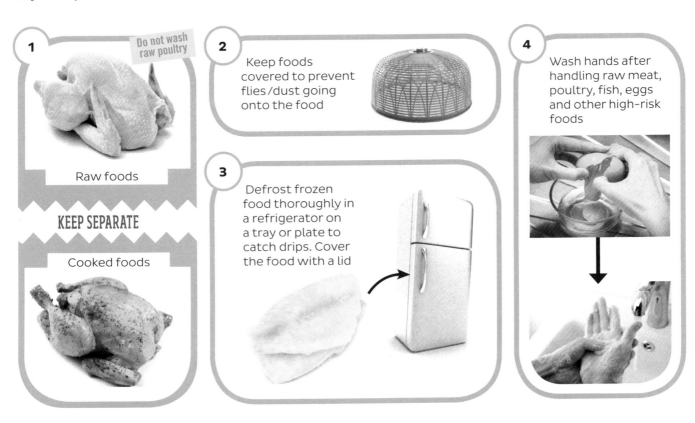

1
Do not wash raw poultry

Raw foods

KEEP SEPARATE

Cooked foods

2
Keep foods covered to prevent flies / dust going onto the food

3
Defrost frozen food thoroughly in a refrigerator on a tray or plate to catch drips. Cover the food with a lid

4
Wash hands after handling raw meat, poultry, fish, eggs and other high-risk foods

They must store, cook, cool and serve food properly:

Storing food

1. Store food correctly as soon as possible after buying it.

2. Do not leave high-risk foods for any length of time in a warm place such as a car boot on a sunny day.

3. Check use-by and best-before dates regularly.
   Use up older foods first. This is called stock rotation.

4. Refrigerators and freezers:
   - Check internal temperatures regularly (0° to 5°C refrigerators, –18° to –22°C freezers)
   - Check door seals are working
   - Defrost regularly to keep them working properly
   - Place away from the cooker or boiler in a kitchen so they can work normally
   - Do not leave refrigerator doors open for any length of time.

Cooking, cooling down and serving food

1. Cook food thoroughly. Check core temperature is at **70°C or hotter** for at least 2 minutes, using a food probe
2. Hot cooked food must be kept at **63°C or above**
3. Left-over hot cooked food should be cooled to **5°C or cooler** within **1½ hours**
4. Left-over cooked food must only be reheated **once** to a minimum core temperature of **70°C** for at least 2 minutes
5. Use **different utensils** to serve different foods to prevent cross-contamination

Using a food probe

1. Reset to zero
2. Sterilise/use antibacterial wipe
3. Insert metal probe into core of food
4. Do not touch hot pan with probe
5. Allow temperature to stabilise (**70°C or hotter for 2 minutes)**
6. Sterilise/use antibacterial wipe after use

Activity 11.1: Hygiene in the kitchen

Scenario: Read the story below about a chef working in the kitchen of a busy cafe.

Find ten things to do with kitchen and personal hygiene that the chef did wrong when he was preparing food.

Sam arrived late at the cafe, so quickly got ready to start work. He forgot to bring a clean uniform to work, so he put on the dirty one he wore all day yesterday, which he had rolled up and put in his locker after work instead of taking it home, because he was going out for the evening. Sam used the toilet and went straight to the kitchen without washing his hands as he didn't want to be told off for being late. He was not feeling particularly well as he had a sore throat, runny nose and kept sneezing.

Sam's first job was to prepare some raw chicken. He could not find the red chopping board, so used a yellow one instead. He sneezed three times and wiped his nose on his sleeve, because his hands were too messy from preparing the chicken to get a tissue out of his pocket.

After preparing the chicken, Sam wiped his hands on a wet dishcloth, which he then used to wipe the worktop and the chopping board. He left the chicken in an uncovered tray on the worktop. His next job was to prepare thirty six raw eggs that would be used later to make omelettes. Sam cracked the eggs into a bowl, whisked them and wiped his hands on his apron. He left the whisked eggs in a bowl next to the chicken he had prepared. He then went straight on to his next job, which was to make some salad.

Sam took the salad ingredients from the boxes in the store room and prepared them on a green chopping board. Some of the lettuce had soil on the leaves, which Sam brushed off with his fingers.

Sam then had a coffee break and as it was a warm, sunny day, he went outside and sat on the rubbish bins in the yard behind the cafe. After his break, he returned to the kitchen and noticed a few flies round the uncovered chicken, so brushed them off with his hands and put the chicken in the refrigerator.

3. Food Labelling Regulations

Book link pp98–99

Food labels tell (inform) people about the food they are choosing to buy.

In the UK, food labelling is controlled by law by:

- **Department of Health** – nutritional labelling
- **Food Standards Agency** – food safety labelling

Food labels must be:

- Clear and easy to read
- Easy to understand
- Easy to see
- Truthful about the food inside.

By law, the following information must be shown on a food label:

1 Nutrition information
2 Ingredients that are known food allergens
3 List of ingredients (in descending order of amount)
4 The quantity of certain ingredients
5 The name of the food product
6 A description of the food product if it is not obvious to the consumer from the name what the food product actually is
7 Indication of minimum durability (the shelf-life of the food product) by 'use-by' or 'best-before' date
8 The weight/quantity of the food product
9 Place of origin (provenance) of the food product or a specific ingredient
10 Cooking or usage instructions
11 Storage conditions and instructions
12 Contact details of food product manufacturer, distributor or retailer

5 **Savoury quiche**

Egg and cheese flan with broccoli and red pepper in a shortcrust pastry case

2 **Allergy Information:** Contains milk, egg, gluten (wheat flour)

1 **Nutritional Information:**

Nutrient	Per 100g	Per serving (90g)
Energy	1038kJ/248kcal	934kJ/223 kcal
Fat of which:	15g	13.5g
Saturates	6g	5g
Monounsaturates	5g	4.6g
Polyunsaturates	2.7g	2.4g
Carbohydrate of which:	21g	19g
Sugars	1.8g	1.6g
Starch	18.2g	16.5g
Fibre	1g	0.7g
Protein	8g	7g
Salt	0.5g	0.4g

Serves 6
7 Use by 15 March
8 Net weight 540g
9 Made with British grown broccoli

3 **Ingredients:** wheat flour, vegetable fat spread, whole milk, eggs, cheddar cheese, broccoli (15%), red pepper (10%), seasoning, flavourings.

10 **Cooking instructions:** Oven: remove outer packaging and place on an oven tray. Heat for 20 minutes at Gas 4/180°C. Can be eaten cold.

11 **Storage instructions:** Keep refrigerated between 0°C and below 5°C. Consume by the use-by date. Can be frozen. Follow star ratings on your freezer.

12 **Contact information:** Made in the UK by Freshly Foods, London. www.freshlyfoods.uk

9 78190 8682 78 9

Knowledge check – can you remember....?

1. One way that food safety laws protect consumers?
2. One way that food safety laws protect food businesses?
3. Two things that all food businesses must do under the Food Safety Act?
4. Two things that all food businesses must do under the Food Hygiene Regulations?
5. What HACCP is?
6. Three examples of critical control points in a food business?
7. Three things that food premises must be?
8. Three personal hygiene rules that food handlers must follow?
9. Two rules about cooking food safely?
10. Two rules about food labels?

E-assessment practice questions

Short answer questions

1. State two ways in which food safety laws protect consumers [2 marks]

2. Food hygiene regulations require food businesses to use a food safety management system called HACCP.
   a) What does HACCP stand for? [1 mark]
   b) Explain what is meant by critical control points [1 mark]
   c) Who will check that a food business is obeying food safety laws? [1 mark]

3. Food storage is a critical control point in food production. It is very important that food is stored correctly to keep it safe to eat.
   a) What will happen to bacteria in chilled foods if they are not stored at the right temperature (i.e. too warm)? [1 mark]
   b) State three controls and checks that a food business should use to prevent a food safety risk in frozen and refrigerated foods [3 marks]

Stretch and challenge question

The temperature of food during cooking, serving, chilling and storage is a critical control point. Food probes are often used in a kitchen to check the temperature of foods.

a) Justify why a food probe should be used to check the temperature of food [1 mark]

b) Explain how to use a food probe to check the temperature of some oven-baked chicken legs [5 marks]

c) Describe how you should safely cool, store and re-use left-over cooked meat curry [4 marks]

Role and responsibilities of Environmental Health Officers

 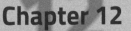

Chapter 12

What do you need to know? **AC4.2**

- How the law protects people who buy food (consumers) from food poisoning
- How the law makes sure that there are high standards of food safety in the food industry

Book link
pp100–103

LO4 Know how food can cause ill health

Key learning

In the UK, Environmental Health Officers (EHOs) are employed by local authorities.

EHOs carry out inspections in businesses where food is sold to the public.

EHOs investigate complaints from members of the public about food businesses.

EHOs also investigate complaints from members of the public and employees about non-food problems in H&C businesses.

The Food Standards Agency sets out what EHOs have to do during inspections to make sure that food businesses follow food safety laws.

Why are food businesses inspected by EHOs?

Book link
p100

Inspections of food businesses are carried out to make sure that:

Food is stored, handled and cooked hygienically and safely

Pests cannot contaminate the food

Food is safe to eat

The food business building is in good condition and regularly cleaned

Food handlers are trained in food safety

Food handlers have good personal hygiene

The food business is using HACCP

What does an EHO do during the inspection of a food business?

Book link
pp100–102

By law, an EHO can:

Enter a food business without an appointment for an on-the-spot inspection

Look at all the records the business keeps, e.g. staff training, refrigerator temperatures, etc.

Check the use-by and best-before dates on foods being stored in the business

Take food away if it is unsafe to eat

Take food samples away to test for bacteria

Tell the business to make hygiene improvements by a certain date

Close the business immediately if it is dangerous to the health of customers

Watch how the food is handled during storage, preparation, cooking and serving

Take photographs/videos of what is seen during an inspection

Environmental Health Officers also investigate:

- Complaints about a food business
- Outbreaks of infectious disease
- Complaints about poor standards of health and safety in H&C businesses

Their other duties include:

- Giving evidence to a judge if a business is taken to court for breaking the law
- Granting licences to food businesses
- Deciding the hygiene rating for a food business
- Giving talks at public enquiries, meetings and exhibitions
- Educating and training people about food safety and environmental health

Activity 12.1: What would the Environmental Health Officer do?

For each scenario below, choose one or more of the actions that the EHO could carry out to deal with the situation.

Scenario 1

A member of the public has contacted the EHO to complain that they have been ill with food poisoning after eating a meat pie from a takeaway shop three days ago.

Scenario 2

A member of the public reports seeing several rats on and near some rubbish bins that belong to a restaurant. The bins are reported to be overflowing with food waste.

Scenario 3

During an on-the-spot inspection of a restaurant kitchen, the EHO finds the following:

- Cooked rice being kept on the kitchen floor in a bucket covered with a dirty cloth
- Mouse droppings in food preparation bowls and on the shelves
- Several staff wearing very dirty kitchen uniform
- Uncovered raw chicken being stored next to (and touching) cooked meat pies in a refrigerator that has an internal temperature of 11°C

Raw chicken

Scenario 4

A small bed and breakfast business is reported to the EHO by a customer who has stayed the night there. The customer was concerned about:

- A leak of sewage at the back of the toilet onto the floor in the bathroom he used
- Patches of black mould on the walls and ceiling of the bedroom he stayed in
- Being bitten by bed bugs during the night
- Being served his cooked breakfast on a cracked plate and being given a fork that had dried food stuck between the prongs

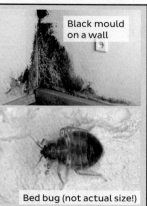

Black mould on a wall

Bed bug (not actual size!)

Actions that an EHO could carry out:

1. Visit the business without an appointment to carry out an inspection.

2. Ask for evidence of illness (e.g. a letter from a doctor) from the person who has made a complaint against a food business.

3. Take food samples away to test for bacteria.

4. Take samples of water, pests, faeces, etc., away to identify and test, and use as evidence.

5. Check that the business is using pest-control equipment, e.g. traps, wire meshes, fly killers.

6. Take photographs / videos of what is seen during an inspection.

7. Look at all the records the business keeps, e.g. staff training, refrigerator temperatures, maintenance of equipment and plumbing, etc.

8. Remove (seize/confiscate) food being sold by the business, because it is unsafe to eat.

9. Tell the business to make hygiene, food safety or other improvements by a certain date.

10. Close the business immediately because it is unsafe for customers to buy food/stay there.

Knowledge check – can you remember....?

1. Four reasons why food businesses are inspected by Environmental Health Officers?

2. Four things that Environmental Health Officers can do by law when they inspect a food business?

3. What an Environmental Health Officer can do if the food business is dangerous to the health of customers?

4. What an Environmental Health Officer can do if there are a few things that need improving in a H&C business?

E-assessment practice questions

Short answer questions

1. State three reasons why Environmental Health Officers inspect food businesses
   [3 marks]

2. State three things that an Environmental Health Officer is allowed to do by law during the inspection of a food business *[3 marks]*

3. Apart from inspecting food businesses, Environmental Health Officers have other duties. State two other duties that they have *[2 marks]*

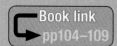
Hospitality and catering provision for specific requirements

Book link
pp104–109

LO5 Be able to propose a hospitality and catering provision to meet specific requirements

What do you need to know? **AC5.1** **AC5.2**

- How to choose (propose) the types of hospitality and catering that you think would be most suitable for the needs of different groups of people, situations and places
- How to set out your choices (your proposal) clearly
- How to give good reasons (justify / give a justification) for the hospitality and catering choices you have suggested

Remember!

Always read a question carefully and several times before you start to answer it.

Make sure you understand what the question is asking you to do.

Highlight any key words in the question so you do not miss out anything in your answer.

Key learning

One of the questions in the Unit 1 e-assessment will give you a scenario to read. A scenario describes the specific needs of different groups of people who are in a particular place (location) for a particular reason (occasion).

To answer the question, you will need to be able to do the following:

1. Write out clearly the types of hospitality and catering choices that you think would be most suitable for the needs of the people described in the scenario.
2. Give good reasons (justify) for your choices

Here is a list of hospitality and catering choices:

 AC5.1 **Book link** pp104–105

Hospitality choices

- Hotels: budget (low cost), five-star, spa, luxury, hotel resort, boutique (small, in tourist areas), business, eco-friendly
- Bed and breakfast businesses
- Hostels
- Caravan and campsites, family cabins
- Clubs and casinos
- Sports stadiums
- Concert/gig venues
- Visitor and tourist attractions, e.g. theme parks, museums, historical buildings, spas, aquariums, safari parks, gardens and parks
- Holiday camps

Catering choices

- Cafes, tea rooms and coffee shops (self-service or waited at table)
- Takeaway and fast food outlets
- Restaurants and bistros
- Canteens and dining rooms
- Pubs and bars
- Mobile/roadside food vans; street food stalls; pop-up restaurants
- Self-catering facilities
- Play/activity centres with cafes
- Set meal, carvery meal, salad bar, buffet, picnic hamper, self-service cafe, takeaway, barbeque, packed lunch

Remember!

These are the types of **residential** hospitality places (where people stay overnight):

Hotels, guest houses, bed and breakfast, inns, pubs, farmhouses, holiday camps and parks, family cabins, luxury camping (glamping), cruise ships, long-distance trains, airlines, motorway services, youth hostels.

These are the types of **catering** places:

Restaurants, bistros, dining rooms, canteens, cafes, tearooms, coffee shops, takeaway and fast food outlets, pubs, bars, clubs, casinos, street food stalls, pop-up restaurants, mobile/roadside food vans, motorway services, visitor and tourist attractions (theme parks, museums, zoos, etc.), sports stadiums, concert/gig venues, hospitals, schools, prisons, care homes, people's homes (for parties, funerals, etc.).

Here is an example scenario

A new eco theme park is being planned. It will have an environmentally friendly theme.

As well as entertainment and rides, the theme park will include an education centre and residential accommodation. Residential courses will be offered all year round to schools, youth groups, college students, families with young children and adult tourist groups.

Question: Suggest and justify one type of hospitality and one type of catering place (establishment) that are suitable to meet the needs of the following groups who want to stay at the eco theme park:

a) Families on holiday with young children

b) School and college students on a residential course.

Suggestions about how you could answer the question

In the example answers below, the following are highlighted in the colours shown:

1. Write out clearly the hospitality and catering choices that you think would be most suitable for the needs of the people described in the scenario.

2. Give good reasons (**justify**) for your choices.

a) For families on holiday with young children, I suggest small family cabins that have a living room, self-catering kitchen, bathroom and two or three bedrooms, with a small outside area for the children to play in. These would be suitable places to stay, because the parents can look after the children in a separate building, without having to worry about disturbing other people. They can cater for themselves if they want to, which would be cheaper than eating out all the time and easier with very young children, who may not eat very much in one meal.

If they decide to eat out, I suggest that a family-friendly restaurant, which sells reasonably priced adult- and child-sized meals in a buffet-style food service system, throughout the day and evening, would be suitable. The restaurant could be divided into separate dining areas, to make eating out together more family-centred and cosier. This would enable families to afford to eat out and give the parents a break from preparing meals. The restaurant could include an indoor play area for children, to allow the adults to relax a little while enjoying their meal, as well as baby-changing rooms and highchairs to make the care of their children more convenient.

b) For school and college students on a residential course, I suggest that hostel accommodation (either in one building or in separate purpose-built buildings) would be suitable. This would have bedrooms for four people to sleep, each with an en suite bathroom. This would enable staff who are in charge to keep a check on a small number of children/students in each room, rather than having them all in one large room. There would be a common room/sitting room, and a dining room/meeting room with a small kitchen facility for groups to prepare simple breakfasts, drinks and snacks. This would allow the children/students to meet together, relax, have whole group meetings and complete any work they have to do for the course.

For their lunches and evening meals, I suggest that the hostel accommodation area includes a separate dining room suitable for large groups. The meals could be served in a cafeteria food service system, which would allow for different needs and food choices. There would be a pre-order packed lunch service available. This would be a convenient way to give the groups a lunch if they are out all day on their courses.

The question might also ask you to give some other information about the scenario and your hospitality and catering choices, e.g.:

Information that might be asked for	Examples of information that you could give for families with young children for the example scenario of an eco-theme park
1. What are its Unique Selling Points (USPs)? What features of your H&C choices will stand out and be attractive to families with young children?	• The accommodation will have everything that is needed for a family (it will be self contained), including adults and children with disabilities • There are suitable activities for different ages of children • There are suitable places to eat that are reasonably priced • The theme park will help people to understand the importance of environmental sustainability • A social media group will be set up to promote special events and offers to previous customers who subscribe to it

2. How does it fit in with current trends in the H&C industry?
 	
What are the current consumer trends and how will your H&C choices meet these?
	• In all its accommodation, restaurants, education centre, etc., the eco-theme park will aim to:
	  – Use mainly renewable energy
	  – Use as little plastic as possible
	  – Recycle water and materials
	  – Keep food waste to a minimum
	  – Cater for disabled customers and those with special dietary needs

3. How will it be promoted? How will customers be attracted?	• An advertising plan – local newspaper; postal drop of leaflets; posters sent to schools, colleges, nurseries and play groups, tourist information centres • Interactive website featuring information about the theme park, accommodation, food, how it aims to be environmentally friendly, etc. • Promotional deals – e.g. discounts (cheaper prices) for group bookings and reduced prices for children under three years old
4. How will the theme park operate? Which staff will be needed and how the business will meet the requirements of the law	• Staff will need to be employed for jobs such as cleaning and preparing the accommodation; working in the family-friendly restaurant; maintenance of the theme park; providing entertainment for families and children • Documents and certificates will need to be kept up-to-date for health and safety, food safety, licences, insurance, fire, gas and electricity safety and water quality

Activity 13.1: Choosing hospitality and catering for different scenarios

For each scenario below, write brief notes about:

- The hospitality and catering choices that you think would be most suitable for the needs of the people described in the scenario
- Reasons (justification) for how your choices meet the needs of the people in the scenarios

Scenario 1

A golden (50 years) wedding anniversary celebration for a couple and their family of three children and eight grandchildren and great-grandchildren (aged 2 years to 18 years)

Scenario 2

A fundraising event to raise money for sports facilities for disabled children and young people, in a town that has a Premier League football team with its own large stadium.

Scenario 3

A charity that supports elderly people has approached the local council with a proposal to open a lunch club in the town centre, in which local elderly residents could meet other people socially and be able to buy inexpensive meals and drinks.

Chapter 14

Assessment of Unit 1: Preparing for the e-assessment

Book link
pp110–123

Remember!

Always read a question carefully and several times before you start to answer it.

Make sure you understand what the question is asking you to do.

Highlight any key words in the question so you do not miss out anything in your answer.

PLEASE NOTE:

This assessment is also available as a written examination, where you write your answers down in pen on the examination paper. Your school may decide to choose the written examination instead of the online version. Check with your teacher.

What do you need to know and understand?

- What an e-assessment is all about
- How the e-assessment is set out
- The words and information that are used for the instructions and questions in the e-assessment
- The different types and styles of questions that are used in the e-assessment
- Useful hints and tips to help you do your best in the e-assessment

Key learning

The e-assessment is an online, external assessment (exam) which is worth 40% of the whole qualification. It is similar to an ordinary written exam, except that instead of using a pen and paper, you use a key pad and a computer to read and answer the questions.

Each question will have one or more text boxes into which you will type your answers. These boxes get longer the more you type, so you will not run out of space.

Some questions may ask you to click on a picture and drag it to a box you choose as your answer.

Once you have answered the assessment questions on the computer, your answers will be securely uploaded to the examination board (WJEC) to be marked and graded. (This is why it is called an external assessment – it is not marked by your teachers at school.)

The maximum total mark for the e-assessment is 90. Each question will show you how many marks it is worth in brackets [ ]. This will give you an idea of how much you should write for each answer. You must answer all of the questions.

Whether you take the online or the written version of this assessment, you will do it under the usual examination conditions, i.e. in silence and within a set amount of time (1 hour and 30 minutes).

Study tip

Be prepared and ready!

This chapter will help you get ready for your e-assessment.

The e-assessment is worth 40% of your final grade, so it is important to be well prepared for it so that you do your best.

If you are well prepared for it, you will be:

- More relaxed and less nervous
- More confident about answering questions
- More likely to be successful and achieve your potential

This is how the exam will be arranged:

Time allowed: 1 hour and 30 minutes
All questions must be answered
Maximum total mark = 90 marks

Study tip
During the course

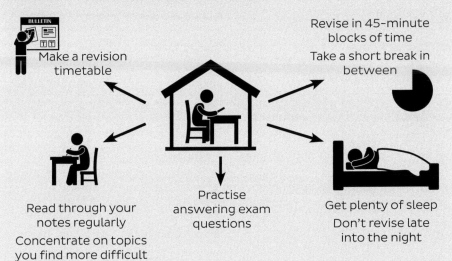

Read your notes after each lesson to check your understanding

If you are unsure about a topic, ask for help

Make revision notes / mind maps / revision cards

Organise your notes and keep them together

Learn each section as you go through the course

Study and revision tips to help you remember a topic more effectively

- 'Teach' a topic to a friend or adult and then test each other
- Get someone to ask you questions about a topic
- Cut down the topic into small pieces of information
- Make a mind map of a topic using key words / colours / pictures
- Make notes with key points / words highlighted
- Make some revision flash cards with key words / definitions on them
- Read the information several times in the weeks before your assessment
- Test yourself with practice questions and quizzes on different topics
- Produce a glossary of key words and terms with their meanings

Study tip
For several weeks before the e-assessment

Make a revision timetable

Revise in 45-minute blocks of time

Take a short break in between

Read through your notes regularly

Concentrate on topics you find more difficult

Practise answering exam questions

Get plenty of sleep

Don't revise late into the night

Study tip
On the day of the examination

Important advice you must follow **before** you start answering the questions in this assessment:

Online e-assessment: Read the front page first as there will be information for you to open a tab or scroll through to find further information or data. There may be a pop-up box for you to click on for details – **MAKE SURE YOU CLICK ON IT!!** (Many students do not do this – don't be one of them!)

Written examination: *Read the instructions on the front page of the examination paper carefully.*

These instructions tell you what you must do to make sure you give your name, school centre number and examination number correctly, and also how to fill in the examination paper with your answers. **MAKE SURE YOU FOLLOW ALL THE INSTRUCTIONS!!**

Write clearly (and not too small), so that the examiner can read your answers – if they cannot read your answers, *they cannot give you any marks*.

For both versions of the assessment: *Read* each question at least **twice** before you start to answer it, to make sure you are absolutely clear about what the question is asking you to do.

What will you be assessed on?

In the e-assessment you will be asked questions about the information you should understand, know and be able to do for each of the following Learning Outcomes (LOs) and their Assessment Criteria (AC) shown in the chart below:

Learning Outcomes	Assessment Criteria: The information you need to be able to answer questions about in the e-assessment	Where to find the information in the Study and Revision Guide	Where to find the information in the student textbook
LO1 Understand the environment in which hospitality and catering providers operate	AC1.1 The structure of the Hospitality and Catering (H&C) industry	Pages 5–13	Pages 8–21
	AC1.2 Job requirements within the H&C industry	Pages 15–17	Pages 22–27
	AC1.3 Working conditions across the H&C industry	Page 18	Pages 26–27
	AC1.4 Factors affecting the success of H&C providers	Pages 20–27	Pages 28–39
LO2 Understand how hospitality and catering provisions operate	AC2.1 The operation of the kitchen	Pages 29–35	Pages 40–51
	AC2.2 The operation of front of house	Pages 37–42	Pages 52–59
	AC2.3 How customer requirements are met	Pages 43–47	Pages 60–65
LO3 Understand how hospitality and catering provision meets health and safety requirements	AC3.1 Personal safety responsibilities in the workplace	Pages 49–51	Pages 66–69
	AC3.2 Risks to personal safety in hospitality and catering	Pages 54–62	Pages 70–75
	AC3.3 Personal safety control measures for H&C provision	Pages 54–62	Pages 70–75
LO4 Know how food can cause ill health	AC4.1 Food related causes of ill health	Pages 64–70	Pages 76–91
	AC4.2 The role of the Environmental Health Officer	Pages 85–86	Pages 100–103
	AC4.3 Food safety laws	Pages 76–84	Pages 92–99
	AC4.4 Common types of food poisoning	Pages 64–70	Pages 76–83
	AC4.5 Symptoms of food related ill health	Pages 64–70	Pages 76–91
LO5 Be able to propose a hospitality and catering provision to meet specific requirements	AC5.1 Review options for H&C provision for specific needs, locations and situations	Page 88	Pages 104–105
	AC5.2 Recommend options for H&C provision for specific needs, locations and situations	Pages 89–91	Pages 106–109

What are command words and what do they mean?

Each question in the e-assessment will have a command word to tell you what you should do to answer it.

The following chart shows you the command words that are used, what they mean and what they require you to do.

Some command words are found in short answer questions and only need a one-word answer, a list or a short sentence. These are shown in the blue shaded areas of the chart.

Other command words are for questions that need a longer answer, where you have to give more information, details and explanations. These are shown in the yellow shaded areas of the chart.

The chart includes some sample questions with the command words highlighted and example answers to give you an idea of what you would be expected to do.

SHORT ANSWER QUESTIONS

Command word	What it means and what you should do	Example question and answer
Identify	To show that you know and understand something by being able to write down its main features and characteristics.	Q **Identify** three items of clothing a chef should wear when working in the kitchen to protect their body and help prevent cross-contamination of bacteria. [3] A i) *A cotton hat that stops hair falling into the food* ii) *A cotton chef's jacket that is double thickness to protect the chest from heat* iii) *A cotton apron that is long enough to cover and protect the legs*
List	Write the information in a list rather than full sentences.	Q **List** three foods that are high risk for being contaminated with food poisoning bacteria. [3] A i) *Raw meat* ii) *Fresh fish* iii) *Raw poultry*
Name	Give the name of something (e.g. a piece of kitchen equipment) or someone (e.g. a job title such as restaurant manager).	Q **Name** the job title for the person who has to perform these roles in a H&C business: • Order ingredients and materials • Store all foods correctly • Keep stock tidy, clean and well organised • Keep a detailed list of all stock [1] A *Stock controller*
Recommend	Write down your idea of what would be suitable for a particular occasion or situation.	Q A new cafe has opened in the centre of a town that is visited by many tourists each year during the summer holiday season. **Recommend** three ways in which the management of the restaurant can continue to attract customers throughout the rest of the year in order to keep the business in profit. [3] A i) *Offer a loyalty scheme for regular customers, such as a card that is stamped each time the customer orders a lunch, and once they have ten stamps on their card, they get one free main lunch course.* ii) *Offer a menu that is served only on one day each week at a discount price, e.g. curries, pies, or a chef's special* iii) *Offer regular discounts to certain target groups, e.g. children under five years old, pensioners, students*
State	Write down a short, clear and accurate list.	Q **State** three personal qualities that a barista in a coffee shop would need in order to make the business a success. [3] A i) *Someone who welcomes customers with a smile and is cheerful* ii) *Someone who knows a lot about what the coffee shop sells so they can help customers make a choice* ii) *Someone who works hard as a team member to make sure all the jobs in the coffee shop are completed and carried out well*

Suggest	Give your ideas/plans to be considered by other people. Give reasons to support your suggestions.	Q **Suggest** two types of food provision that would suit a university campus food hall for students. [2] A i) *A self-service cafeteria, so students can choose what they want and pay at a till* ii) *A multi-point counter service serving different types of food to suit a wide range of student needs, e.g. vegetarian, gluten free, 'grab and go' pre-packed foods, religious dietary rules*

LONGER ANSWER QUESTIONS

Command word	What it means and what you should do	Example question and answer
Describe	Write down the features and details about something or someone. You do not need to explain them.	Q **Describe** the role of a member of the front of house staff in a hotel reception. [4] A *Reception staff work directly with customers, to welcome and check them in and out of the hotel; take them to their rooms; sort out any problems they have; take bookings from new customers; and help customers sort out things such as travel plans and visits to local tourist attractions. They also work as an important link between the customer and the back of house staff to make sure that all customer needs are met.*
Review	Explain and evaluate the importance, quality or value of something.	Q **Review** the importance of a workflow in the operation of the kitchen. [4] A *Workflow means the way and order in which food is produced as it passes through the kitchen, from being delivered as ingredients at the kitchen door, to being served as a complete meal in the dining area. Catering kitchens are busy places, with several people working at the same time in different parts of the kitchen doing different activities to produce a range of different menu items for customers, so it is important that the workflow is planned so that the staff do not waste time and energy by having to walk about too much; nothing gets in the way and stops them working efficiently and the food is produced with as little risk of cross-contamination by bacteria as possible so it is safe to eat.*
Analyse	Look at something carefully and thoroughly and in detail so that you can write about it.	Q **Analyse** why the use of information and computer technology (ICT) is important for the success of H&C businesses. [6] A *Computer technology includes social media, digital technology, mobile smartphones and smart devices that are linked to them (e.g. smart watches), satellite navigation, and the Internet. Research shows that many customers want and expect H&C businesses to provide high-quality and modern products and services, and they want to use environmentally and sustainable services and products. Hospitality and catering businesses can send information about their services directly to customers using ICT, so they can easily find the type of food/accommodation they want, which saves them time and effort. Customers can also make online bookings and orders for food and drink, etc. This helps businesses to know how many customers to cater for, which helps to prevent wastage of food, etc. Satellite navigation helps customers to easily find places to eat or stay in an area and can direct them to the ones they choose. Social media enables customers to instantly review their experiences of a H&C business, which can help increase customer numbers if the reviews are good. Reviews also help H&C businesses to improve their customer services. Comparison websites on the Internet enable customers to compare prices, facilities and services of different H&C businesses, which can help increase customer numbers.*

Justify	Write down the reasons why you think something is better than something else. Give examples/evidence to back up your reasons.	Q	The managers of a city-based youth group for teenagers are organising a one-week outdoor activity holiday in a rural area. Suggest two types of accommodation they could use and **justify** which one you think is the most suitable to meet the needs of the staff and teenagers. [8]
		A	*The youth group could go to:*

a) *A bed and breakfast hotel that could offer packed lunches and evening meals each day for an extra cost.*

Or

b) *A youth hostel that offers bed and breakfast and the use of a self-catering kitchen and dining room.*

Having all meals provided by a hotel would save time and effort, but it is likely that the youth group will have a limited amount of money to spend on accommodation and food, so the youth hostel will probably be better value, because they can save money on meals by self-catering. They could arrange a rota so that every teenager is involved in preparing meals and clearing away, which will teach them some cooking and organisation skills, as well as working together in a team. Self-catering also means that it will be easier to cater for teenagers and staff who may have special dietary needs, such as religious or cultural needs, food allergies or intolerances. The youth hostel will also have special facilities for washing and drying clothes and shoes that are used in the outdoor activities, which might not be the case in a hotel. The dining room in the youth hostel can also be used to hold meetings during the activities holiday. In a hotel, there may be other guests staying at the same time, so it may be difficult to find a suitable space for such meetings.

Explain	Write about something very clearly, giving examples to illustrate your answer, to show that you understand what you are writing about.	Q	Explain the role and importance of Environmental Health Officers in the prevention of food poisoning. [8]
		A	*Environmental Health Officers are employed by local authorities to enforce food safety laws by inspecting businesses where food is sold to the public, e.g. restaurants, cafes, hotels, guest houses, pubs, etc.*

The purpose of an inspection is to make sure that customers who eat food that they buy do not become ill and also to protect the business from customers who make a false claim for food poisoning against it. The Environmental Health Officers will do this by making sure that, for example:

- *Food is being stored, handled and cooked hygienically and safely*
- *Food is not being contaminated by harmful bacteria and is safe to eat*
- *Food handlers have been trained in food hygiene and safety*
- *Food handlers know the importance of personal hygiene (washing hands, clean clothing, etc.)*
- *There are control measures in place to prevent pests such as flies and mice from contaminating food*
- *The place where the food is produced is in good condition and regularly cleaned*

Environmental Health Officers will also:

- *Check to make sure that food safety hazards and risks have been identified and are being controlled by using a food safety management system, such as HACCP*
- *Offer advice to the owners of a food business about staff training and improving food hygiene and safety in the business*

If an Environmental Health Officer finds a problem in a food business, they can:

- *Take food that they think is a food safety hazard (e.g. because it has been stored in a refrigerator that is too warm or has passed its use-by date) away from the business, so that it cannot be sold to customers*
- *Tell the owners of the business to make hygiene and food safety improvements within a set time and come back to make sure that they have done this*
- *Close the business and stop them selling food if there is a high risk of food poisoning, e.g. because the kitchen is very dirty; there is evidence of rats/mice in the kitchen; or high-risk food is being stored incorrectly*
- *Give evidence in a law court if the owners of the business are prosecuted for breaking the law*

What types and styles of questions are used in the e-assessment?

There are various types of questions that are used in the e-assessment:

- Some questions are designed to test your **memory** (recall) of information
- Some questions want you to **apply** what you know and understand to a particular situation
- Some questions want you to write about some **data** that you are given.

Some questions will begin with a **sentence** or **statement** so that you know what the topic of the question is about.

Activity 14.1: Answering questions

The e-assessment will be a mixture of different styles of question, and examples of these are set out below. Have a go at answering them.

Short answer questions

These questions ask you to remember/recall information that you have learned. They often use the following command words:

Identify   List   Name   Recommend   State   Suggest

Q List two job roles for each of the following staff in a hospitality and catering business:
  a) Executive head chef *[2]*
  b) Housekeeper *[2]*
  c) Maintenance manager. *[2]*

Q Identify three factors that affect the success of a hospitality and catering business. *[3]*

Q List four things that affect the profit made by a hospitality and catering business. *[4]*

Q State four things that make good customer service in a hospitality and catering business. *[4]*

Stimulus questions

These questions give you either an image or some words that you have to drag and drop into a box you have chosen as the correct answer, e.g.:

Q   Safety signs are used in H&C businesses to make customers and employees aware of personal safety hazards and risks.

Identify each safety sign by matching the image to the description.
Match the signs to the correct description box: *[4]*

i)   Wear gloves in the freezer room

ii)   Toxic substance

iii)   Emergency escape route this way

iv)   Caution – wet floor

Graduated lead-in questions

The questions start with a written statement which leads into the questions – usually a short answer question followed by two questions that need longer answers, e.g.:

Q   Businesses are increasingly being encouraged to reduce their use of plastics because of their effect on the environment.

a)   Identify two reasons why the use of plastics is bad for the environment. *[2]*

b)   Suggest two ways in which each of the following sectors of the Hospitality and Catering industry can reduce their use of plastics: *[6]*

   i)   Catering kitchens

   ii)   Bars and restaurants

   iii)   Accommodation and housekeeping.

c)   Explain why it is important for the success of a hospitality and catering business to tell their customers how and why they are trying to reduce their impact on the environment. *[2]*

Data response questions

These give you some information (data), which you need to use to answer the questions that follow after it.

Q A motorway services company has produced this data for visitors in a year to one of its service locations that has overnight accommodation, parking spaces for cars and lorries, restaurants, shops, toilet facilities and a fuel station.

a) Describe two types of non-food hospitality services that the company could provide to meet the needs of each of the following visitors who use the motorway services:
  i) Long distance lorry drivers
  ii) Business people *[4]*

b) Suggest three food service options that the company could offer to suit families and overseas visitors *[3]*

c) Review your suggestions for food service options and justify why each would be suitable for the needs of families and overseas visitors *[6]*

Free response questions

These questions are about a topic or scenario, and are often worth quite a few marks. You have the choice about how you are going to answer them, but you must remember to include details, examples and explanations and try not to repeat what you have already written.

Q A new bar and restaurant is opening in a busy town centre. It is in part of an old, disused department store that has been restored and modernised. The restaurant kitchen and customer toilet facilities will be in the basement of the building and there will be a drinks bar and customer tables on the ground floor and first floor.

Describe the safety features that will need to be included in the building to make sure that customers and staff are safe at all times, and how the food will be delivered from the basement kitchen to the customers on the ground floor and first floor in the most efficient way. *[9]*

Activity 14.2: Getting good marks for your answers

In this activity, the same question has been answered by two different students.

When you have read through their answers, say how many marks you would give them if you were the examiner, and explain why.

Here are some guidelines to help you.

Has the student:

● Given a clear or a muddled answer?
● Followed what the command word asked them to do?
● Covered the needs of the stated group of people in their answer?
● Given details and examples in their explanation?
● Given enough information or only a little?
● Given information that is correct or incorrect?

Q A charity is setting up a lunch club for elderly adults in a small town, many of whom live alone and find it difficult to cook for themselves. The lunch club will provide a two-course lunch followed by tea or coffee, and will operate three times a week from a community centre, which has a well-equipped catering kitchen and hall.

a) Suggest two types of food provision that the club could provide to meet the needs of the elderly people [2]

b) Review your suggestions and justify which one you think is the most suitable [8]

c) Suggest and justify two non-food ideas that the club could provide to make the club an enjoyable social occasion for the elderly people [4]

Student 1 answer

a) Suggest two types of food provision that the club could provide to meet the needs of the elderly people. [2]

   i) *Sandwiches and cakes that people choose from a cafeteria*

   ii) *Ready meals that the people choose and are heated up for them*

b) Review your suggestions and justify which one you think is the most suitable. [8]

People like sandwiches and cakes and the elderly people can choose the ones they want, but sandwiches are cold, so they might prefer to have a hot ready meal. The ready meals can be bought in by the lunch club and stored in the freezer, which will save them time as they won't have to cook anything. So the ready meals would be best as they are easy to prepare and the elderly people can choose what they want.

c) Suggest and justify two non-food ideas that the club could provide to make the club an enjoyable social occasion for the elderly people. [4]

   i) *They could play some games, e.g. bingo*

   ii) *They could watch a film*

Student 2 answer

a) Suggest two types of food provision that the club could provide to meet the needs of the elderly people. [2]

   i) *A choice of two cooked meals made in the kitchen and served to the elderly people at their tables (table service system)*

   ii) *A choice of two cooked meals served to the elderly people at the counter (cafeteria system)*

b) Review your suggestions and justify which one you think is the most suitable. [8]

It is important to offer people a choice of meal, e.g. a vegetarian and non-vegetarian meal so that everyone is catered for. However, the charity will have to be careful not to spend too much money on ingredients or waste food, so maybe the elderly people can choose what they want from the menu a few days before, either at the previous lunch club, or a charity volunteer could contact them by telephone. The charity would keep a record of what they choose in case they have forgotten on the day of the lunch club. This will help the charity to plan how much food they need to order and cook in advance.

As many of the elderly people have difficulty cooking for themselves, having a hot meal that is cooked at the club and eating it with other people will be very comforting and sociable for them and will give them greater variety in their diet. It will also be like being at a restaurant, which makes the experience very enjoyable.

I think the most suitable option is to have the meal served to the elderly people at the table, because if they have problems standing and walking, they would find it very difficult to queue up at a counter and carry their tray of food back to their table. This could also be dangerous if one of them slipped and fell.

c) Suggest and justify two non-food ideas that the club could provide to make the club an enjoyable social occasion for the elderly people. [4]

   i) *If there is a piano in the community hall, the charity could ask someone to play background music during the meal (or they could use a sound system instead), and maybe have a popular song singing session at the end of the meal, using songs that the elderly people knew when they were young. Singing is a good activity to help keep elderly people's brains active, as well as being fun.*

   ii) *After the meal, the charity could perhaps set up some tables with board/card games for people to play in groups or for them to sit and chat, in order to extend the social aspect of the club, as this is very important for elderly people who live alone, and it is also another good way of keeping their brains active.*

Chapter 15  Nutrients and water

What do you need to know?

- Why the body needs water and nutrients from food **AC1.1**
- Which foods contain the different nutrients
- What happens if the body does not have the right amount of nutrients or water **AC1.3**
- What happens to nutrients when foods are prepared and cooked **AC1.4**

Book link
pp124–149

LO1 Understand the importance of nutrition when planning menus

Key terms you should try to include in your answers

Balanced diet – a diet that provides a person with the right amount of nutrients for their needs

Diet – the food people eat every day

Good nutrition – eating a wide variety of foods (mainly plant foods), that are mostly unprocessed (whole foods) and drinking plenty of water

Nutrients – natural chemical substances in foods that are essential for body growth, function and health

Nutrition – the study of what people eat and how all the nutrients in foods work together in the body

Key learning

- **Nutrients** are natural substances that are essential for our bodies to grow, work properly and stay healthy.
- Water is not a nutrient, but we cannot live without it.
- **Nutrition** is the study of what people eat and how all the natural substances (including nutrients) in foods work together in the body so it can grow, stay healthy and work properly.
- **Good nutrition** means eating lots of different fresh fruits, fresh vegetables and other plant foods such as wholegrain cereals (wheat, oats, barley, rice, rye), and smaller amounts of fish, meat, poultry, dairy foods and eggs, and drinking plenty of water.
- The food people eat every day is called their **diet**.
- A **balanced diet** gives a person the right amount of nutrients for their needs. There are also special diets, e.g. a low salt diet or a high fibre diet.
- All foods contain different amounts and types of nutrients.
- **Whole foods**, such as whole grain cereals (wheat, oats, rice, etc.), beans and whole milk are **nutrient dense** because they contain the most nutrients. They have not had any nutrients removed by processing.
- **Nutrient-rich** foods contain a lot of a particular nutrient; e.g., fresh orange, kiwi fruit and broccoli are rich sources of vitamin C.

Why the body needs water and nutrients from food

Book link
pp125–131

Nutrient: Protein		Which foods contain it (Sources)
Why it is needed (Function) **AC1.1**	· **Growth** of the body · **Repair** of the body when it is injured · Gives the body **energy**	**Plant foods:** Beans, peas, lentils, cereals (rice, wheat, oats, barley, rye) and cereal products (bread, pasta, etc.), nuts, seeds, soya beans, quinoa, tofu, textured vegetable protein (TVP), Quorn.
What happens if you do not have enough (Deficiency) **AC1.3**	· Children do not grow properly · Hair falls out · Poor skin and nails · Infections · Poor digestion of food	**Animal foods:** meat, poultry, fish, eggs, milk, cheese, yogurt, quark, gelatine.
What happens if you have too much (Excess) **AC1.3**	· Excess stored as fat · Weight gain – obesity · Puts a strain on the liver and kidneys	
What happens to it when food is prepared and cooked **AC1.4**	· The appearance and texture of protein is changed (it is **denatured** and **coagulated**) by heat and acids (e.g. lemon juice) · It can be overcooked, which makes it difficult to digest in the body	

Nutrient: Carbohydrate

Why it is needed (Function) AC1.1	• Main source of **energy** for the body • **Dietary fibre** helps the body get rid of solid waste products (faeces)

Which foods contain it (Sources)

There are two groups of carbohydrates:

Group 1 – sugars:

Glucose: ripe fruits and vegetables (e.g. apples, onions, beetroot, parsnip, sweet potato).

Fructose: fruits, vegetables and honey. (**High fructose corn syrup** (HFCS) is used as a sweetener in many processed foods and fizzy soft drinks.)

Galactose: milk from mammals.

Maltose: barley, a syrup (malt extract), added to breakfast cereals, biscuits, hot drink powders, confectionery (sweets).

Sucrose: 'sugar' from sugar cane and sugar beet and used in cooking and many processed foods, drinks and confectionery.

Lactose: milk and milk products.

What happens if you do not have enough (Deficiency) AC1.3	Rare in the UK and similar countries: • Lack of energy, tiredness • Weight loss • Severe weakness • Not enough fibre – constipation
What happens if you have too much (Excess) AC1.3	• Excess carbohydrate not used for energy is **stored as fat** • Weight gain – obesity • Frequently eating too many **refined and processed carbohydrates** (e.g. white bread, doughnuts, biscuits, cakes, potatoes, white rice, pasta etc.) and **free sugars** (e.g. sugar, sugary foods, sweet soft drinks, biscuits, cakes) can lead to: • Raised blood sugar levels • Type 2 diabetes • Tooth decay
What happens to it when food is prepared and cooked AC1.4	• Starch (carbohydrate) is **gelatinised** when cooked in a liquid, which makes it easier for the body to use • Sugars melt and dissolve in water. As they are heated they boil and turn into a syrup, which **caramelises**. Overheating causes sugars to burn.

Group 2 – complex carbohydrates:

Starch: cereals (e.g. wheat, rice, oats, barley, maize [corn]), cereal products (e.g. breakfast cereals, pasta, bread, cakes, pastry, biscuits); starchy vegetables (e.g. potatoes, yams, sweet potatoes, parsnip, pumpkin, butternut squash, peas, beans, lentils); seeds, quinoa.

Pectin: some fruits, e.g. oranges, lemons, limes, apples, apricots, plums, greengages and some root vegetables, e.g. carrots.

Dextrin: formed when starchy foods (e.g. bread, cakes, biscuits) are baked or toasted.

Dietary fibre / non-starch polysaccharide (NSP): wholegrain (wholemeal) cereals and cereal products, e.g. breakfast cereals, bread, pasta, flour; fruits and vegetables, especially with skins left on (e.g. peas, beans, lentils); seeds, nuts.

Nutrient: Fat

Why it is needed (Function) AC1.1	• Gives the body **energy** which is stored in the body under the skin and elsewhere • **Insulates** the body from cold temperatures • **Protects** the bones and kidneys from physical damage • Gives the body **'fat soluble' vitamins A, D, E, K**

Which foods contain it (Sources)

Plant foods:
Plant oils, e.g. olive, rapeseed, palm, coconut, sunflower and corn; and also oily fish, avocados, nuts, seeds and some vegetable fat spreads.

Animal foods:
Oily fish, eggs, fresh meat, poultry, milk, butter, cream, cheese, lard, suet, ghee, the fat in meat, and chocolate.

What happens if you do not have enough (Deficiency) AC1.3	Rare in the UK, but deficiency causes: • Weight loss • Feeling cold • Bruising of bones if knocked • Lack of vitamins A, D, E, K
What happens if you have too much (Excess) AC1.3	Common in countries like the UK and causes: • Excess stored in the body as fat • Weight gain – obesity, which can lead to heart disease and cancers • Excess fat is also stored elsewhere inside the body, e.g. around the intestines, liver and other vital organs, which stops them working properly • Excess fat stores can lead to diseases such as obesity, diabetes, heart disease, high blood pressure, shortage of breath
What happens to it when food is prepared and cooked AC1.4	• Fats and oils are damaged by repeatedly being heated to fry foods • They break down into substances that are harmful to the body

Visible fats and oils:
Fats/oils in a food that you can easily see: e.g. fat in meat, oil in tuna, butter, lard, suet, block vegetable fat, ghee, plant oils such as olive, palm, sunflower oil.

Invisible fats and oils:
Fats/oils in a food that you cannot easily see: e.g. in cakes, pastries, potato crisps, chips, biscuits, chocolate, nuts, cheese, fried foods, meat products, etc.

Activity 15.1: Make a poster

Choose **one** of the following nutrients, and design and draw an A3-size poster to explain clearly why the body needs it and which foods it is found in. Make the poster colourful and clearly set out so that it attracts people to read it:

Protein   Fat   Carbohydrate   Vitamin C   Vitamin D   Iron   Calcium

Nutrient : VITAMINS	Why the body needs it (Function) AC1.1	Which foods contain it (Sources)	What happens if you do not have enough (Deficiency) AC1.3	What happens if you have too much (Excess) AC1.3	What happens to it when food is prepared and cooked AC1.4
Vitamin A	For healthy skin To see in dim light To help children grow To keep mucus membranes in the body moist and prevent infections Antioxidant which helps prevent heart disease and cancers	**Animal foods (Retinol):** milk; cheese; butter; eggs; liver, kidney; oily fish, vegetable fat spreads (added by law). **Plant foods (Beta carotene):** cabbage, spinach, kale, lettuce; peas; orange/yellow/red vegetables and fruits (e.g. carrots, apricots, mango, papaya, peppers, tomatoes)	Dry and infected skin and mucus membranes Night blindness leading to total blindness Poor growth in children	Poisonous if too much taken, e.g. in supplements, especially to unborn babies	Not affected
Vitamin D	Helps the body absorb calcium Helps calcium add strength to bones and teeth	Sunlight on skin; oily fish, meat, eggs, butter, vegetable fat spreads (added by law), fortified breakfast cereals	Bones weaken and bend: called rickets in children and osteomalacia in adults	Rare	Not affected
Vitamin E	Antioxidant which helps prevent heart disease and cancers	Soya, corn oil, olive oil, nuts, seeds, whole wheat, vegetable fat spreads	Rare	Rare	Not affected
Vitamin K	Helps blood clot after injury	Green, leafy vegetables, liver, cheese, green tea	Rare but may happen in newborn babies	Rare	Not affected
Vitamin B_1	Allows energy to be released from carbohydrates	Meat, especially pork; milk, cheese, eggs, vegetables, fresh and dried fruit, wholemeal bread, fortified breakfast cereals, flour	Beri-beri – affects nerves and muscles	Rare	Damaged by heat and dissolves in water
Vitamin B_2	Allows energy to be released from carbohydrates, fats and proteins	Milk and milk products, eggs, fortified breakfast rice, mushrooms	Rare – sore corners of mouth	Rare	Damaged by heat and dissolves in water
Vitamin B_3	Allows energy to be released from carbohydrates, fats and proteins	Beef, pork, wheat flour, maize flour, eggs, milk	Pellagra – diarrhoea, dementia, dermatitis	Rare	Damaged by heat and dissolves in water
Folate (Vitamin B_9)	Makes healthy red blood cells Helps prevent spinal cord problems in unborn babies	Green leafy vegetables, yeast extract (e.g. Marmite), peas, chickpeas, asparagus; wholegrain rice, fruits, added to some breads and breakfast cereals	Anaemia Possibly spina bifida in newborn babies	Rare	May be damaged by high heat
Vitamin B_{12}	Makes healthy red blood cells Makes healthy nerve cells	Liver, meat, fish, cheese, fortified breakfast cereals, yeast	Anaemia	Rare	May be damaged by high heat
Vitamin C	Helps the body absorb iron Maintains connective tissue to bind body cells together Antioxidant which helps prevent heart disease and cancers	Fruits and vegetables, especially citrus fruits (e.g. oranges, lemons, limes and grapefruit), blackcurrants, kiwi fruit, guavas, Brussels sprouts, cabbage, broccoli, new potatoes, milk and liver	Anaemia Bleeding under skin Loose teeth Wounds do not heal Scurvy	Rare	Damaged by heat and dissolves in water Damaged when exposed to the air

Activity 15.2: Which vitamin?

Look at the chart below and work out which vitamin each set of pictures is about.
Explain how you worked out the answers from the picture clues.

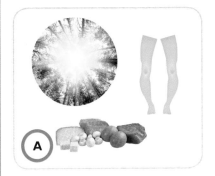

A

B

C

D

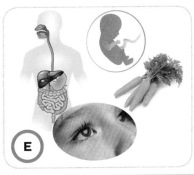

E

Nutrient : MINERALS	Why the body needs it (Function) AC1.1	Which foods contain it (Sources)	What happens if you do not have enough (Deficiency) AC1.3	What happens if you have too much (Excess) AC1.3	What happens to it when food is prepared and cooked AC1.4
Calcium	To make strong **bones and teeth** Makes **nerves and muscles** work Helps **blood clot** after injury	Milk, cheese, yogurt; green leafy vegetables; canned fish; some nuts, enriched soya drinks; flour	Bones and teeth weaken Bones bend Nerves and muscles don't work properly Blood will not clot after injury	Rare Calcium may build up in the soft tissues of the body	Not affected
Iron	Makes **haemoglobin** in **red blood cells** to carry **oxygen** to all body cells and produce **energy**	Red meat, kidney, liver; wholemeal bread, added to wheat flour (except wholemeal); green leafy vegetables (e.g. watercress, spinach, cabbage); egg yolk; dried apricots; lentils; cocoa, dark, plain chocolate; curry powder; fortified breakfast cereals	Iron deficiency anaemia Tiredness and lack of energy Weakness Pale skin complexion Weak and spilt nails	Too much is poisonous if taken, e.g. in supplements	Not affected
Sodium	Controls **water** in body Makes **nerves and muscles** work properly	Salt (**sodium** chloride); salted foods; cheese, yeast extract, stock cubes, gravies and seasonings, snack foods (e.g. crisps), canned fish, bacon, ham, dried fish, soy sauce, salted butter, fast foods and many ready meals; baking powder (cakes, biscuits, baked desserts); takeaway foods	Muscle cramps	Too much sodium (salt) leads to high blood pressure and cardio-vascular disease	Not affected

Fluoride	Strengthens **tooth enamel** and bones	Seafood, fish, tea, some water supplies	Weak enamel – more chance of tooth decay	Too much fluoride may lead to discoloured teeth	Not affected
Iodine	Makes **thyroxin** in thyroid gland to control **metabolic rate** of body	Seafood, vegetables, dairy foods	Swelling in neck (goitre)	Rare	Not affected
Phosphorus	Strong **bones and teeth** **Energy** release Makes **cell membranes** especially in the brain	Wide range of foods	Rare	Rare	Not affected

Activity 15.3: Which mineral?

Look at the chart below and work out which mineral each set of pictures is about. Explain how you worked out the answers from the picture clues:

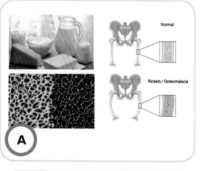

A

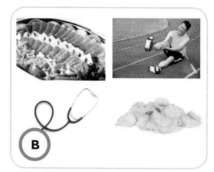

B

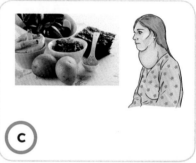

C

D

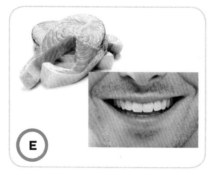

E

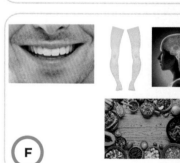

F

Water

Why the body needs water (Function) AC1.1	Which foods contain water (Sources)	What happens if you do not have enough water (Deficiency) AC1.3	What happens if you have too much water (Excess) AC1.3
Controls body temperature Needed for chemical reactions in the body Removes waste products from the body Keeps mucous membranes moist and healthy Keeps skin moist and healthy Needed for all body fluids Found in all body cells	Drinking water (tap water) Naturally found in many foods – milk, milk products, fruit, vegetables, meat, fish, eggs Added to many foods – soup, sauces, pastries, breads, boiled rice, pasta, beans, pulses, etc.	You become thirsty You get a headache **Dehydration** – the urine becomes very dark in colour You feel weak and sick The body overheats You become confused The blood pressure and heart rate change	Substances in the blood become over-diluted Vital organs in the body start to fail, e.g. heart, kidneys May cause death

What do you need to know? **AC1.2**

- How dietary guidelines aim to help people choose what to eat
- The nutritional needs of people at different life stages
- Which foods people can/cannot eat when they are on a special diet or have a medical condition
- Energy needs for different levels of activity

Book link
pp134–139

LO1 Understand the importance of nutrition when planning menus

Key learning

What are the dietary guidelines?

Book link
p134

Dietary guidelines are **recommendations** (from a government organisation called Public Health England) about what to eat in order to be healthy.

There are eight recommendations:

1. Base your meals on starchy foods
2. Eat lots of fruit and vegetables
3. Eat more fish – including a portion of oily fish each week
4. Eat less saturated fat and sugar
5. Eat less salt – no more than 6g (1 level teaspoon) a day for adults
6. Get active and be a healthy weight
7. Don't get thirsty – drink plenty of water
8. Don't skip breakfast

They are shown in an illustration called the Eatwell Guide:

Key term you should try to include in your answers

Life stages – stages of development that people go through during their life: i.e. infancy (babyhood), childhood, adolescence (teenagers), adulthood and later adulthood (elderly people)

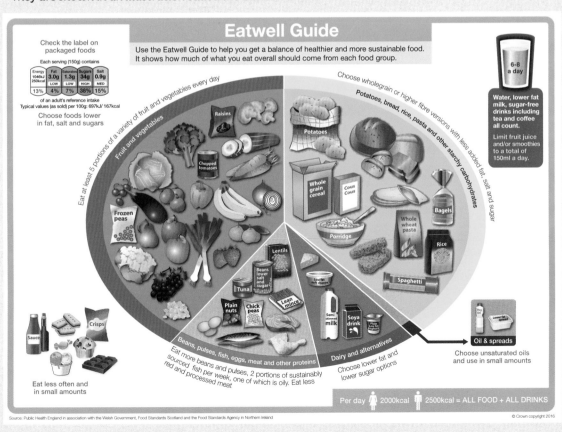

Eatwell Guide

Use the Eatwell Guide to help you get a balance of healthier and more sustainable food. It shows how much of what you eat overall should come from each food group.

Source: Public Health England in association with the Welsh Government, Food Standards Scotland and the Food Standards Agency in Northern Ireland

© Crown copyright 2016

Activity 16.1: Why are dietary guidelines recommended?

Using your knowledge of nutrients in foods, match the dietary guidelines with the correct reason why each is recommended:

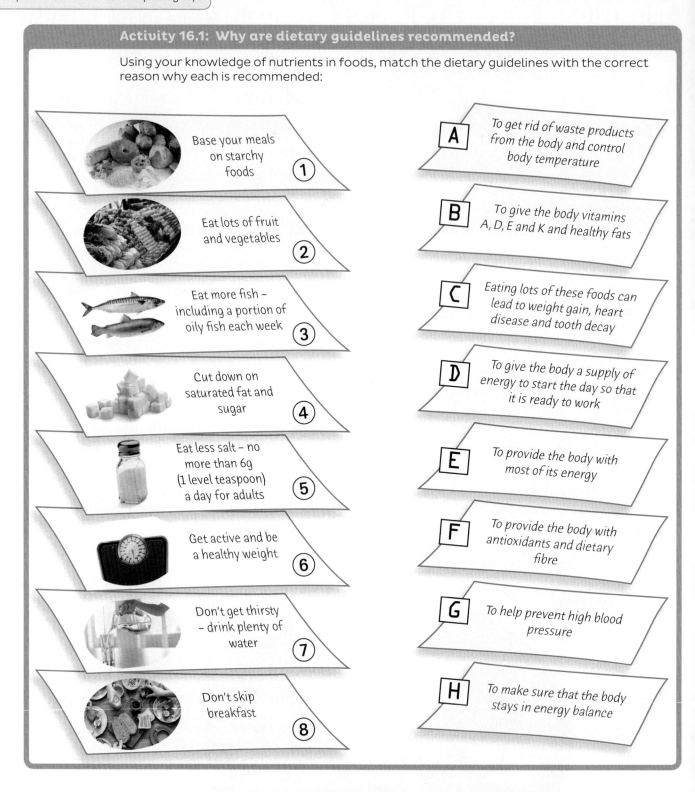

Base your meals on starchy foods (1)

Eat lots of fruit and vegetables (2)

Eat more fish – including a portion of oily fish each week (3)

Cut down on saturated fat and sugar (4)

Eat less salt – no more than 6g (1 level teaspoon) a day for adults (5)

Get active and be a healthy weight (6)

Don't get thirsty – drink plenty of water (7)

Don't skip breakfast (8)

A To get rid of waste products from the body and control body temperature

B To give the body vitamins A, D, E and K and healthy fats

C Eating lots of these foods can lead to weight gain, heart disease and tooth decay

D To give the body a supply of energy to start the day so that it is ready to work

E To provide the body with most of its energy

F To provide the body with antioxidants and dietary fibre

G To help prevent high blood pressure

H To make sure that the body stays in energy balance

Key terms you should try to include in your answers

Free sugars – sugars, honeys, syrups and fruit juices/fruit concentrates that are added to foods and drinks by manufacturers, cooks/chefs and consumers to sweeten them during preparation, processing, cooking and serving

Peak bone mass – when bones and teeth have the maximum amount of minerals and are at their strongest and most dense

What are the nutritional needs of people at different life stages?

Book link
pp135–136

Life stage	Which nutrients/foods are especially important?
Pre-school children 1–4 years • Fast body growth and development • A lot of energy is used in physical activity	• All nutrients, especially protein, vitamins and minerals • Limit the amount of **free sugars** and salt in foods and drinks
Children 5–12 years • Growth continues in 'spurts' • Children should be physically active most of the time to prevent them becoming overweight or obese	• All nutrients, especially protein, vitamins and minerals • Limit the amount of free sugars and salt in foods and drinks
Adolescents (teenagers) • Fast body growth and development from a child into an adult • Minerals are put into the bones and teeth, so the skeleton reaches **peak bone mass** when they are adults	• Protein, vitamins A, B group, C, D, E, carbohydrate (starch and fibre; limit free sugars) • Fats – especially essential fatty acids • Minerals – all • Calcium and vitamin D
• Girls start to have periods, which means they may become anaemic	• Iron and vitamin C
• Not enough sleep and pressures of school may lead to lack of energy, poor concentration and tiredness	• Vitamin B group, Iron and vitamin C
Adults • The body stops growing around 21 years of age • The body needs to be looked after to prevent disease, and be strong and active • Can gain weight if the diet is unbalanced and they are not physical active	• Protein, vitamins A, B group, C, D, E, carbohydrate (starch and fibre; limit free sugars), fats – especially essential fatty acids, minerals – all
• Peak bone mass is reached around 30 years of age	• Calcium and vitamin D
• Women continue to have periods until the menopause (approximately late 40s to early 50s), which may mean they become anaemic	• Iron and vitamin C
Older adults • Body systems such as digestion, blood circulation, etc., start to slow down • Blood pressure may increase • The body needs to be looked after to prevent disease, and be strong and active • Can gain weight if the diet is unbalanced and they are not physical active • The appetite usually gets smaller • The senses of smell and taste may weaken	• Protein, vitamins A, B group, C, D, E, carbohydrate (starch and fibre; limit free sugars), fats – especially essential fatty acids, minerals – all • Iron and vitamin C: (especially women) to avoid scurvy and anaemia
• Short- and long-term memory may become poor	• B group vitamins: to help the body use energy and to help prevent memory loss
• The eyesight may weaken	• Vitamins A, C and E: to help prevent age-related eye condition
• Bones and teeth gradually start to lose minerals and become weak. This can develop into osteoporosis.	• Calcium/vitamin D

These graphs show how some nutrient needs change at different life stages, and why this happens:

Amount of protein (g) needed per day

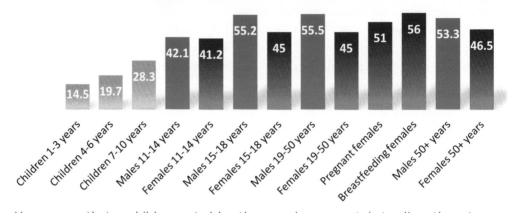

You can see that as children get older, they need more protein to allow them to grow. When they are teenagers they have big growth spurts, so they need even more protein, but as they become adults and have finished growing, they need less. Pregnant and breastfeeding females need more protein to allow the baby to develop and grow.

Amount of calcium (mg) needed per day

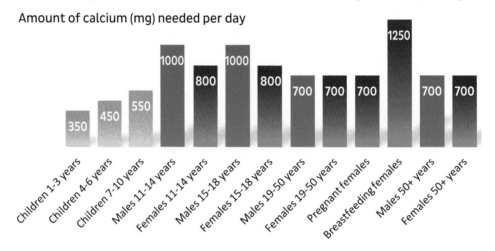

You can see that as children get older, they need more calcium (and vitamin D) to allow their bones and teeth to grow and become stronger. When they are teenagers they have big growth spurts, so they need even more calcium, but as they become adults and have finished growing, they need less, but enough to allow them to reach peak bone mass so that their bones and teeth are really strong. Pregnant and breastfeeding females need more calcium to allow the baby's bones and teeth to develop and grow.

Amount of iron (mg) needed per day

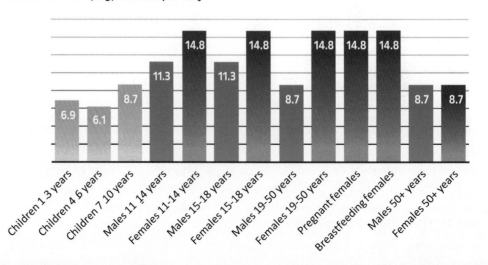

You can see that as children get older, they need more iron (and vitamin C) to produce enough red blood cells to take oxygen around the body and produce energy in all body cells. When they are teenagers they have big growth spurts and many are physically active and need plenty of energy, so they need even more iron. Females need more iron than males because they lose blood when they have their periods and the iron that is lost must be replaced. As they become adults, females continue to need the same amount of iron because their periods continue, but males need less. Pregnant and breastfeeding females need more iron than males because they need enough to enable the baby to develop and grow and to make sure they have enough for themselves to prevent them from becoming anaemic. As males and females reach older adulthood, they need less iron (the same amount as each other) because women do not have periods after the menopause.

Amount of vitamin A (mcg) needed per day

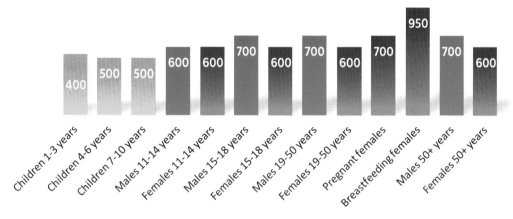

You can see that as children get older, they need more vitamin A to allow them to grow normally, fight disease, and keep their eyes, skin and mucous membranes healthy. When they are teenagers their need increases and stays the same throughout their adult life. Breastfeeding females need more vitamin A to allow the normal development of their baby.

Special diets for different food choices and medical conditions

Book link
p137

What they do eat	Reason(s) for following this diet	What they do not eat
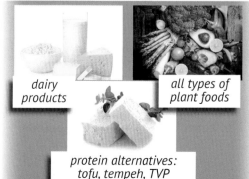 dairy products / eggs / all types of plant foods	**Lacto-ovo vegetarian diet** Health, religious, ethical (what people believe is the right thing to do), or other	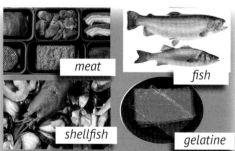 meat / fish / shellfish / gelatine
 dairy products / all types of plant foods / protein alternatives: tofu, tempeh, TVP	**Lacto vegetarian diet** Health, religious, ethical or other	 meat / fish / gelatine / shellfish / eggs

all plant foods

protein alternatives: tofu, tempeh, TVP

all animal foods

fish and shellfish

dairy products and eggs

Vegan diet

Health, religious, ethical, environmental or other

rice, rice products, soya

maize (corn), cassava (tapioca)

linseeds, polenta, beans, peas

lentils, quinoa, sorghum, agar, nuts

wheat and wheat products

bread, cakes

biscuits, pastries

barley, oats, rye products

Gluten-free diet

To prevent symptoms of coeliac disease

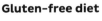

specially produced lactose-free dairy foods

milk, milk products, and any food containing milk products

Lactose-free diet

To prevent symptoms of lactose intolerance

fruits, vegetables

wholegrains

rice, peas

beans, lentils

white flour and products

white rice

smooth fruit juice

High fibre diet

To prevent the development of diseases of the intestines, e.g. constipation, diverticular disease

fresh fruits and vegetables

milk, unsweetened milk products

free sugars that have been added to cakes, biscuits, drinks, confectionery, desserts, sauces, ice cream, breakfast cereals, honey, syrup, jam, etc.

Low sugar diet

To control the symptoms of diabetes; as part of a diet to lose weight

naturally low-fat foods, e.g. fruits vegetables, cereals, white fish, fat reduced cheese, spreads, milk, etc.

Fat reduced diet
To prevent the development of heart disease; as part of a diet to lose weight

full-fat dairy foods, pastries, meats, crisps, chips, doughnuts, cakes, biscuits, fried foods, desserts, ice cream

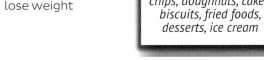

Low sodium (salt) diet
To prevent the development of heart disease, high blood pressure, kidney disease

fruits, vegetables, milk, eggs

yeast extract, cheese, dried fish, canned fish, soy sauce, ketchup, pickles, many ready meals and takeaways, snack foods, cakes, biscuits, scones

Nutritional needs for different activity levels

Book link pp138-139

Energy is needed for different jobs in the body. Energy comes from food and is converted to **glucose** in the body to give us energy.

If a person is physically active they are less likely to develop diseases such as obesity and heart disease. Being physically active also improves the strength of the bones and muscles and keeps the brain active and alert.

Physically active people need enough food every day to give them sufficient energy for their **BMR** and their **PAL**.

People who are not very physically active (sedentary people), need to limit the amount of energy they have from food in order to prevent them putting on weight.

The mind map on the next page will help you understand about the body and energy.

Key terms you should try to include in your answers

BMR – basal metabolic rate is the amount of energy we need to keep our body alive

Energy balance – the amount of energy we get from food each day is the same as the amount of energy we use each day

Energy dense – a food that contains a lot of fat and/or carbohydrate (sugar, starch) and has a high energy value

PAL – this means physical activity level, and is the amount of energy we use for movement and physical activity every day

A revision mind map to help you learn about energy:

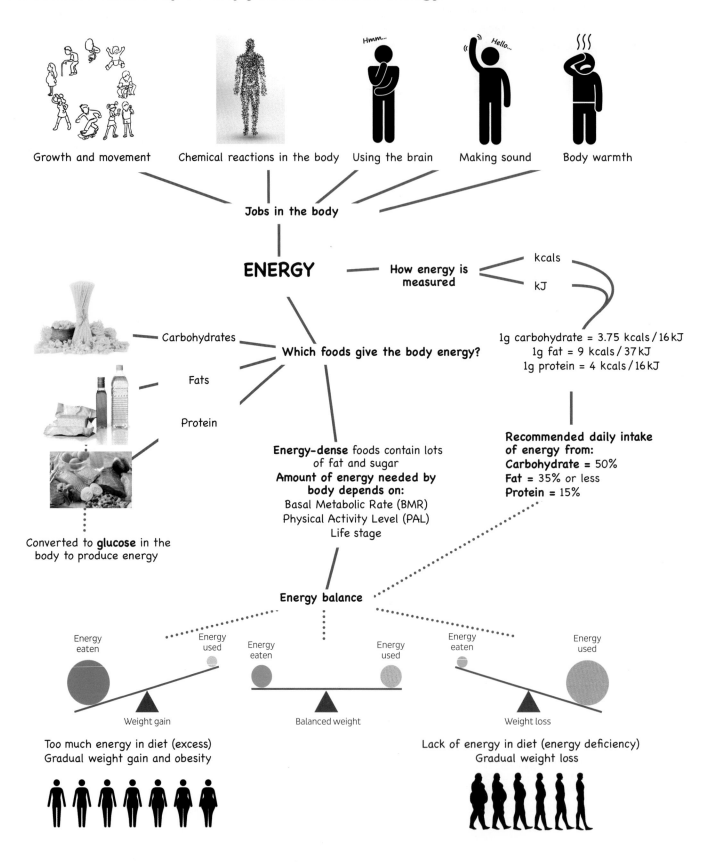

Growth and movement   Chemical reactions in the body   Using the brain   Making sound   Body warmth

Jobs in the body

ENERGY

How energy is measured

kcals

kJ

Carbohydrates

Fats

Protein

Which foods give the body energy?

1g carbohydrate = 3.75 kcals / 16 kJ
1g fat = 9 kcals / 37 kJ
1g protein = 4 kcals / 16 kJ

Converted to **glucose** in the body to produce energy

Energy-dense foods contain lots of fat and sugar
Amount of energy needed by body depends on:
Basal Metabolic Rate (BMR)
Physical Activity Level (PAL)
Life stage

Recommended daily intake of energy from:
Carbohydrate = 50%
Fat = 35% or less
Protein = 15%

Energy balance

Energy eaten   Energy used   Energy eaten   Energy used   Energy eaten   Energy used

Weight gain   Balanced weight   Weight loss

Too much energy in diet (excess)
Gradual weight gain and obesity

Lack of energy in diet (energy deficiency)
Gradual weight loss

Activity 16.2: Which foods are energy dense?

Look at the pictures in the chart and work out which ones **are energy dense** or **are not** energy dense.

For each one you say is energy dense, explain why the ingredients it contains make it energy dense.

For each one you say **is not** energy dense, explain why it is not.

	Energy dense or not energy dense?	Explain why you have given this answer
cucumber and lettuce		
jam doughnut		
chocolate chip cookie		
low fat strawberry yogurt		
pork pie		
lentil and vegetable soup		
chips, cheese and mayonnaise		
kebab and fries		
sausage roll made with puff pastry		
fresh fruit salad		

Chapter 17

Menu planning

What do you need to know? **AC2.1** **AC2.2**

Book link
pp150–153

LO2 Understand
menu planning

- How catering businesses choose dishes when planning menus
- How the production, processing, cooking and eating of food affects the environment of the Earth

Key learning

- The different types of menu
- What a menu should tell customers about the food they are choosing
- What to think about when planning a menu
- Why careful menu planning is important
- Food and its effects on the environment
- How to plan menus for dishes (food items) that have the least effect on the environment when they are prepared and cooked.

Different types of menu

Book link
pp150–153

A menu is a list of dishes to choose from.

Many catering businesses have different menus that are changed each day, week or month. This adds variety for regular customers and is more interesting for the chefs.

Types of menu:

A la carte: a menu where the dishes are all listed and priced separately under different headings

Cyclic menu: a set of menus with limited choices that are changed every week, two weeks or month

Du jour menu: a menu that changes each day or is only served on a certain day of the week

Function menu: similar to table d'hôte, but with a more limited choice and used for functions such as weddings, parties and conferences

Meal menu: menu choices for specific meals: breakfast, brunch (late breakfast / early lunch), lunch, afternoon tea, dinner (evening meal). Often used in hotels and in some restaurants and cafes

Speciality menu: for target groups of people, e.g. children, pensioners, ethnic groups, special diets. Used in fast food outlets, some restaurants and cafes

Table d'hôte: a set menu with limited choices, which has a set price for a meal (e.g. a two- or three-course meal)

Activity 17.1: Which type of menu?

Using the types of menu chart above to help you, match each type of menu to the correct image:

A A la carte	**B** Cyclic menu	**C** Du jour menu	**D** Function menu
E Meal menu	**F** Speciality menu	**G** Table d'hôte	

1

Spice up your day with our
CURRY CLUB
£4.49
Every Thursday all day
TUCK IN!
Your choice of curry and a drink from the selection on the menu

2

Small Businesses Conference 2019

Menu
Vegetable soup (v)
Seafood cocktail

Mains
Grilled chicken salad
Vegetable curry with rice (v)
Fish pie with seasonal vegetables

Desserts
Fresh fruit salad with cream
Apple pie with custard or cream
Salted caramel cheesecake
Selection of cheeses and crackers

3

	Week 1	Week 2
Monday	Margherita Pizza Vegetable Bolognaise Jacket Potato with Tuna Mayo Carrots & Garden Peas Fruit Crumble with Custard Yoghurt/Fresh Fruit Platter	Margherita Pizza Quorn & Vegetable Rice Jacket Potato with Tuna Mayo Roasted Peppers & Sweetcorn Berry & Apple Strudel & Custard Yoghurt & Fresh Fruit Salad
Tuesday	Spaghetti Bolognaise (made with Organic Mince Beef) Vegetable Pasta Bake Filled Baguette with Ham/Cheese/Tuna or Egg Sweetcorn & Broccoli Chocolate & Beetroot Brownie Yoghurt/Fresh Fruit Salad	Chicken Fajita with Jacket Wedges Macaroni Cheese Filled Baguette with Ham/Cheese/Tuna or Egg Peas & Coleslaw Lemon Drizzle Cake Yoghurt/Fresh Fruit Platter
Wednesday	Roast Gammon with Roast Potatoes & Gravy Quorn Roast with Roast Potatoes & Gravy Jacket Potato with Beans Seasonal Vegetables Cheese & Biscuits Jelly/Fresh Fruit Platter	Roast Pork with Roast Potatoes & Gravy Vegetable Pasty with Roast Potatoes Jacket Potato with Beans Seasonal Vegetables Cheese & Biscuits Oaty Cookie/Fresh Fruit Salad

4

- Kids' Corner -
For children 12 and under.

Funny Face
A big chocolate chip pancake with a whipped topping smile, buttermilk version available upon request 2.79
Panqueque Cara Graciosa

★ Silver Five
Five silver dollar-sized buttermilk pancakes with an egg and bacon 2.99
Cinco de Plata

Egg Sandwich
One egg, one strip of bacon and cheese on a toasted English muffin. Served with hash browns 2.79
Sandwich de Huevos

★ Rooty Jr.²
Kid-sized version of our famous Rooty Tooty. One egg, one bacon strip, one pork sausage link and a fruit-topped buttermilk pancake. 2.99

Cheese Omelette
With two buttermilk pancakes 3.99
Tortilla de Huevos con Queso

French Toast
Two triangles of French toast with two bacon strips 2.79
Tostija

Pigs in Blankets
Two pork sausage links rolled in buttermilk pancakes and served with hash browns 2.79
Salchichas Enrolladas en Panqueques

Chicken Strips
With french fries 3.99
Tiras de Pollo

Hamburger
Served with fries in a basket 2.99
With cheese 2.99
Hamburguesa

Grilled Cheese Sandwich
Served with French fries 2.99
Sandwich de Queso a la Plancha

Drinks
Soft Drinks, Milk, Chocolate Milk, Hot Chocolate .99
Bebidas

Dessert
Ice Cream Sundae 1.39
Postres

5

6

Menu
2 courses £21
3 courses £25

Starters
Soup of the day
Liver pâté with Melba toast
Avocado salad (v)
Prawn cocktail

Mains
Chicken curry with rice and seasonal vegetables
Vegetable quiche flan with salad and new potatoes (V)
Braised beef with creamed potatoes, and seasonal vegetables
Grilled fillet of lemon sole, new potatoes, samphire and carrots

Desserts
Two scoops of local ice cream served with a wafer and fruit coulis
Gooseberry crumble with custard or cream
Vanilla cheesecake
Selection of cheeses and crackers

7

Special Lunch Time Menu
Monday to Friday 11am - 3pm

Traditional Scottish Fayre	Single	Supper
Fish	3.50	4.00
Chicken	3.50	4.00
Sausage	2.60	3.00
Haggis	2.60	3.00
Black Pudding	2.60	3.00
King Rib	2.60	3.00
Smoked Sausage	2.60	3.00
Steak Pie	2.60	3.00
Mince Pie	2.20	3.00

Chips	
Chips	1.60
Chips & Cheese	3.00
Chips & Curry /Gravy	3.00
Chips, Cheese & Curry	3.40
Deep Fried Mars Bar	2.00

Pizzas	
Pizza Slice & Can	3.00
10" Pizza & Can	4.50

Sandwiches	
Cheese	2.30
Ham & Cheese	2.60
Tuna Mayo	2.60
Salami & Cheese	2.60
Ham & Salami	2.95

Baguettes	
Ham & Cheese	2.60
Pastrami & Cheese	2.60
Salami & Cheese	2.60
Ham & Salami	2.95

Pasta	
Lasagne	3.30
Spaghetti Bolognese	3.50
Macaroni Cheese	3.30
Penne Picante	3.50
Spaghetti Carbonara	3.50

What a menu should tell customers

Book link p150

A menu should:
- Be easy to read and understand
- Be clearly set out
- Have clear descriptions / images of the dishes.

A menu should also give customers the following information:

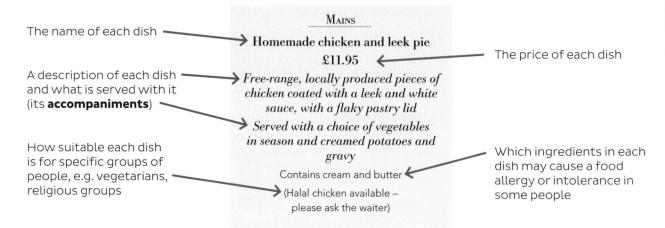

The name of each dish → **MAINS**

Homemade chicken and leek pie
£11.95 ← The price of each dish

A description of each dish and what is served with it (its **accompaniments**) → *Free-range, locally produced pieces of chicken coated with a leek and white sauce, with a flaky pastry lid*

Served with a choice of vegetables in season and creamed potatoes and gravy

How suitable each dish is for specific groups of people, e.g. vegetarians, religious groups

Contains cream and butter ← Which ingredients in each dish may cause a food allergy or intolerance in some people

(Halal chicken available – please ask the waiter)

Planning a menu AC2.1

Book link p153

When planning a menu, a H&C business needs to think carefully about:

1. Customers

- What types of food do they need?
- What types of food do they want to eat?
- What is their age group?
- How much are they willing to pay for food?
- What are their cultural and religious food needs?

2. The business

- Will the menu make money (a profit)?
- Is there enough equipment available to make the menu?
- Will the menu attract new customers?
- How and where would the menu be served, e.g. in a restaurant; as room service; in a bar?

3. How the menu would be prepared

- Is there enough space to store, prepare and serve all the items on the menu?
- Are there enough skilled staff?
- Is there enough time to prepare the menu?
- How will food safety be guaranteed?
- How will the menu be prepared in a way that is environmentally sustainable?

4. The dishes

- Is there a variety of colour, texture and flavour in the menu?
- Is there a variety of foods in the menu?
- Are the foods of a good quality?
- Are all the ingredients available to buy?
- How many of the dishes use locally grown, seasonal ingredients?

The benefits of careful menu planning

Book link
p154

A carefully planned menu will benefit the different parts of a H&C business in the following ways:

The customers

- Interesting, balanced and varied menus can be offered
- Plenty of choices for people with special dietary needs and wants can be offered
- Healthy choices for different groups of people can be offered

The success of the business

- The budget can be planned accurately
- The menu will attract customers
- The business will keep up-to-date with current food trends
- The menu will help to increase profits

The menu

- Ingredients and materials can be ordered in good time
- Local and seasonal foods can be used
- The business will be prepared for busy times, e.g. annual festivals such as Christmas, Diwali and special occasions and seasons e.g. Valentine's Day, summer weddings, tourist season
- Having alternative menus ready in case there are problems, e.g. with buying ingredients

The preparation of the dishes on the menu

Being able to plan ahead for:

- How and in what order the menu will be cooked (make a production plan)
- Who will prepare each dish
- What equipment will be needed
- How the dishes will be presented and served
- Which dishes can be made in advance and reheated

Menu planning and the environment (AC2.2)

 Book link pp156–161

Food production has a major effect on the environment:

PRODUCTION

The production of meat and dairy foods produces the most greenhouse gases

Making and using lots of man-made fertiliser pollutes land, water and air

PROCESSING & MANUFACTURE OF FOOD PRODUCTS

Uses a lot of non-renewable energy and water

Keeping food cold in refrigerators and freezers uses a lot of non-renewable energy and produces greenhouse gases

FOOD PACKAGING

A lot of plastics and paper are used in food packaging

Many plastics do not break down (they are not biodegradable) so must be dumped in land fill or burnt, which causes pollution

Plastic production uses a lot of non-renewable energy (oil) and produces greenhouse gases. Many plastics are not recycled and are causing serious harm to animals and plants in the oceans and on land

TRANSPORTING FOOD

Many foods and ingredients are transported very long distances (called **food miles**)

Air, sea and land transport use a lot of non-renewable energy (oil) and cause pollution

All use non-renewable energy (coal, oil) and produce **GREENHOUSE GASES**
e.g. CO_2, methane, nitrous oxide

Greenhouse gases trap heat and warm the planet

Higher or lower than normal temperatures

which causes **climate change**

Drought (lack of water)

Extreme storms

Flooding

The effects of climate change:
— Crops fail
— Livestock die
— Soil and nutrients blown or washed away
— Land and farm buildings damaged
— Pollination of crops affected
— Landslides and forest fires cause loss of land, crops and livestock
— Water, soil and land polluted by sewage, rubbish, stones during flooding
— Temperature changes cause insects and moulds to grow in large numbers
— Some plant species die out with climate change

How to plan menus that have the least effect on the environment

Ingredients

H&C businesses should try to:

- Use ingredients that have been grown locally and have only travelled a short distance
- Plan the menus so that the food can be delivered to the kitchen in as few journeys as possible, e.g. buy food in bulk; buy from one supplier
- Use foods that are in season, so that they do not have to be imported from other countries
- Use (where possible) ingredients that have been grown organically or are 'free range' (where animals and birds are able to live outside).

Packaging

H&C businesses should try to:

- Use ingredients that have as little packaging as possible
- Use ingredients such as spices, flavourings, sauces etc., that come in refillable or recyclable catering-sized containers
- Avoid serving dishes with individually packaged portions of sauces, salad dressings, salt and pepper, butter and other spreads, jams, marmalade, etc.

Food storage and preparation

H&C businesses should try to:

- Make sure refrigerators and freezers are placed in cool areas of the kitchen – if they are in hot areas, their motors have to work very hard, which uses more energy
- Make sure the refrigerator/freezer door seals are in good condition, so that warm air is kept out
- Avoid opening the door of the refrigerator or freezer too often or leaving it open
- Avoid putting hot food into a refrigerator or freezer – cool it down first
- Defrost refrigerators and freezers regularly to make sure they work efficiently.

Cooking food

H&C businesses should try to:

- Make sure that oven door seals are in good condition, as they help prevent heat being lost from the oven
- Fill up the oven with items to cook to make full use of the energy used to heat it
- Cook more meals on the hob – make sure that the pans fit properly over the gas flame / electric ring to prevent heat escaping
- Keep pan lids on to cut down heat loss
- Use an electric induction hob, microwave oven or slow cooker where possible, which all use small amounts of electricity
- Use quick methods of cooking, e.g. stir frying, sautéing, to cut down on the amount of gas/electricity used
- When cooking several types of vegetables, place them in different sections of a tiered steamer, so only one hob ring is used to cook them.

Wonky veg

Food waste

H&C businesses should try to:

- Avoid buying too much food by planning menus as accurately as possible
- Avoid serving very large food portions to cut down on food waste
- Store food correctly so it stays fresh
- Make use of oddly-shaped fruits and vegetables that are often cheaper to buy and are just as nutritious and well flavoured
- Serve some fruits and vegetables with their skins left on to avoid unnecessary food waste
- Send food waste to be turned into compost so that it can be used to grow more plants
- Use left-over cooked and uncooked foods to make other dishes
- Send left-over food to charities who collect it for people in need.

Activity 17.2: Preventing food waste

Think of some dishes you could make using these left-over foods:

Left-over food	Your suggestions for dishes you could make
1. Cooked chicken breast	
2. Cooked carrots and potatoes	
3. Cooked beef Bolognese sauce	
4. Cold cooked pork sausages	
5. Fresh fruit salad	
6. Cooked pasta	
7. Uncooked mushrooms that are starting to go wrinkly	
8. Some fresh chopped tomatoes, half an onion, some slightly wilted basil leaves and two cloves of garlic	

Menu planning: Meeting customer needs

Chapter 18

What do you need to know? **AC2.3**

- How to plan menus that meet customer needs
- How to make menus attractive and tempting for customers

 **Book link** pp162–167

LO2 Understand menu planning

Key learning

Menus should be **balanced**, which means they should have:

A variety of dishes at different prices

A variety of foods

A variety of cooking methods

A range of nutrients (nutritionally balanced)

A variety of dishes from different cultures

Menus should meet customers' needs

 Book link pp162–166

Nutritional needs

Many customers want healthy food for themselves and their children. Ideally, the menu should follow dietary guidelines (see page 107), by including a variety of dishes that use the recommended amounts of foods that people need to be healthy, i.e.:

Mostly:

Vegetables and fruit

Complex carbohydrates (rice, potatoes, pasta, bread)

Some:

Proteins (beans, peas, lentils, eggs, meat, poultry/fish)

Dairy foods (milk, cheese, yogurt, cream)

Only a small amount:

Fats and oils

Only sometimes:

Foods such as chocolate and savoury snacks

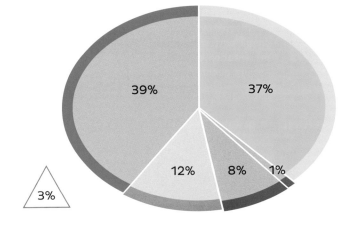

Special dietary needs

The menu should offer some dishes that suit people on special diets, e.g.:

- Dairy free
- Gluten free
- Nut free
- Low salt, low sugar, low fat
- High fibre
- Vegetarian/vegan
- Religious dietary laws, e.g. Jewish people do not eat pork or shellfish; Hindus do not eat beef.

Alternative foods could be offered for people on special diets, e.g.:

- Soya or nut milk instead of cow's milk
- Gluten free bread rolls
- Wholemeal bread instead of white bread
- A vegan version of a menu item
- Boiled or baked potatoes instead of fried chips.

Sensory needs

Eating food is one of life's pleasures and to enjoy it, all the body's senses (**sight, smell, taste, touch** and **sound**) need to work together.

Menu planning, food preparation, cooking and serving should be carried out really well so that the dishes that are produced are **appetising** (people want to eat them) and appeal to all the senses.

The following mind maps and text explain how the senses affect customer enjoyment of food, and how to plan menus to appeal to customer senses. There are also examples of words that describe foods, some of which are used in menus.

How to plan and prepare dishes on a menu that appeal to customers' senses

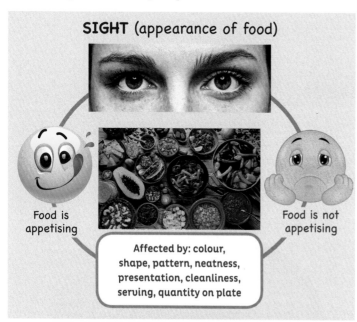

SIGHT (appearance of food)

Food is appetising

Food is not appetising

Affected by: colour, shape, pattern, neatness, presentation, cleanliness, serving, quantity on plate

Present, decorate and garnish food neatly and creatively

Make use of colours – natural food colours, serving dishes, table settings

Cut, shape and form food into decorative shapes and presentations

Make sure plates and dishes are cleaned before serving the food, to remove drips and splashes

Make sure the foods fits on neatly on the plate or dish

Words to describe how food looks (appearance): appetising, neat, colourful, decorative, fresh, frothy, bite-sized, charred, comforting, glazed, glossy, healthy

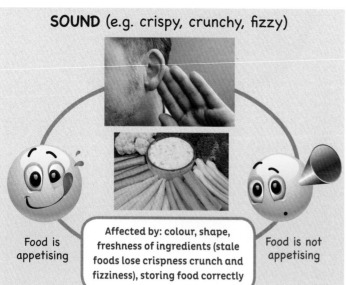

SOUND (e.g. crispy, crunchy, fizzy)

Food is appetising

Food is not appetising

Affected by: colour, shape, freshness of ingredients (stale foods lose crispness crunch and fizziness), storing food correctly

Plan menus to include a variety of textures

Store food correctly so it stays fresh and keeps its texture and sound, e.g. salad foods should be stored in a cool place; dry foods, such as biscuits, should be kept in an airtight tin away from moisture so that they stay crisp

Cook foods correctly to develop their texture and therefore their sounds

Words to describe how food sounds: crispy, crunchy, crackling, fizzing, hissing, snap, bubbly, popping, sizzling

SMELL (aroma of food)

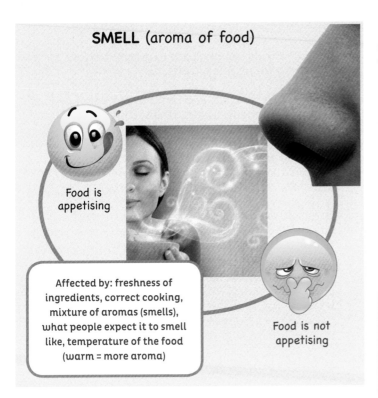

Food is appetising

Food is not appetising

Affected by: freshness of ingredients, correct cooking, mixture of aromas (smells), what people expect it to smell like, temperature of the food (warm = more aroma)

Use a mixture of foods to produce a variety of aromas (smells), but do not using too many, as the overall effect will be spoiled

Make sure that food is cooked properly – aromas are released when food is heated, but they can easily be spoiled if the food is overcooked

Make sure that only fresh ingredients are used – stale foods do not make good aromas

Use natural foods that produce strong (robust) aromas, e.g. fresh and dried herbs and spices, garlic, orange, lemon and lime zest; and cooking methods that develop aromas, e.g. grilling, roasting, baking, sautéing, frying

Words to describe how food smells (aromas): fresh, fragrant, savoury, sweet, pungent (a strong smell), rancid ('gone-off' food), sour, aromatic (pleasant), fruity, fishy, citrusy (like lemons/oranges), earthy (like mushrooms), stale, piquant (strong, makes the nose tingle, e.g. vinegar)

TASTE (flavour of food)

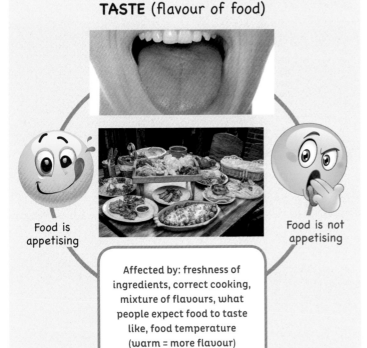

Food is appetising

Food is not appetising

Affected by: freshness of ingredients, correct cooking, mixture of flavours, what people expect food to taste like, food temperature (warm = more flavour)

Use fresh food – stale food loses its flavour

Cook food carefully to avoid damaging flavours, e.g. overcooking can make some flavours become bitter, such as those in spices, butter and green vegetables

Use cooking methods that 'bring out' (develop) flavours, e.g.:

- Sautéing vegetables in butter or oil
- Making stock from meat, poultry or fish bones plus vegetables, herbs, peppercorns and other spices
- Roasting root vegetables (e.g. carrots, beetroot, onions, garlic, parsnips), which makes flavours stronger (concentrates/intensifies the flavour) by allowing water to escape from them (evaporate) and caramelises the natural sugars they contain
- Reducing a sauce (allowing water to evaporate by heating it) so that its flavours become stronger

Use natural flavours, e.g. citrus fruit zest, fresh herbs and spices, e.g. rosemary, sage, basil, ginger and lemongrass

Do not add too much when using strong flavours such as chilli, fish sauce and soy sauce, as they can easily overpower other flavours and make the food unpleasant to eat

Do not add too many other flavours to delicately flavoured foods such as fish

Try mixing a few different flavours, but be careful: too many flavours together may not work

⚠ *Remember!*
Always taste food before you serve it so you can check the flavour and change it a little if needed.

⚠ *Remember! FOOD HYGIENE!*
Do not taste the food and put the spoon you have licked back into the food without washing it first!

Words to describe how food tastes (flavours): salty, umami (savoury/meaty), sweet, sour, bitter, bland (very little flavour), spicy, herby, peppery, nutty, smoky, tangy, yeasty, acidic

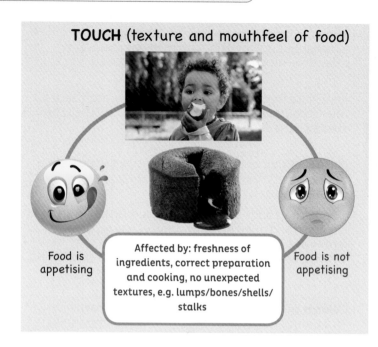

TOUCH (texture and mouthfeel of food)

Food is appetising

Food is not appetising

Affected by: freshness of ingredients, correct preparation and cooking, no unexpected textures, e.g. lumps/bones/shells/stalks

Plan menus that include a variety of textures

Use fresh foods – stale foods lose their texture quite quickly, e.g. vegetables, fruits, fish

Prepare food carefully and remove parts that cannot be eaten, e.g. shells, bones, stalks, tough skins, fruit stones and seeds, small stones and grit

Cook food well to avoid unexpected textures, e.g. lumps in a sauce, undercooked egg white, undercooked cake mixture, overcooked and tough meat

Cook food at the correct temperature and for enough time to allow textures to develop, e.g. when melting chocolate, baking a cake or bread, frying doughnuts

Words to describe how food feels (textures): chewy, creamy, crispy, crumbly, crunchy, crusty, doughy, melt-in-the-mouth, flaky, puffy, fluffy, juicy, moist, succulent, sticky, gooey, smooth, tender, oily/greasy, mushy, frothy, spongy

Activity 18.1: Planning menus to meet customers' sensory needs

Look at the three-course dinner menu below. Identify and describe which parts of the dishes particularly appeal to the different senses – an example is given to show you.

Menu/Dish	Sight	Smell	Taste	Touch	Sound
Starter: Lentil and tomato soup	Red/orange colour of the soup. Green parsley and cream garnish		Fresh tomatoes, garlic, sautéed onion and celery add flavour	Cooked lentils thicken the soup. Smooth texture produced by liquidising the soup. Croutons add crunchy texture	
Served with baked garlic croutons *(made from bread, melted butter, crushed garlic, salt and pepper)*					
Main course: Thai chicken curry. Sticky rice. Steamed green beans					
Dessert: Molten chocolate surprise puddings *(sponge pudding with hidden chocolate that melts during cooking and pours out when opened by a spoon)*					
Served with vanilla ice cream and fresh raspberries					

Activity 18.2: How would you make these dishes look more appetising

Suggest some ways that you could make the following dishes look more appetising and creative:

| Tomato soup |  | |

| Cauliflower with cheese sauce (cauliflower au gratin) |  | |

| Spaghetti Bolognese |  | |

| Grilled chicken |  | |

| Plain sponge cake |  | |

| Plain crème caramel |  | |

| Plain panna cotta |  | |

Include a variety of dishes to cater for different likes and dislikes

Do the dishes on the menu appeal to customers' senses – sight, smell, taste, touch and sound?

Offer suitable portion sizes for different needs, e.g. children, older adults, active people

Offer some dishes that would suit different health conditions

Show customers which dishes may not be suitable for them if they have food allergies or food intolerances

LACTOSE FREE

Things to take into account when planning menus to meet customer needs

Offer some dishes to suit different customer lifestyles, e.g. active / inactive / a busy family / an office worker, etc.

Offer some dishes that would suit a range of religious or cultural dietary rules

Are the prices of dishes on the menu affordable for the target customers?

Think about the type of meal to be eaten – everyday or special occasion, packed meal, etc.

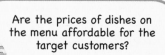

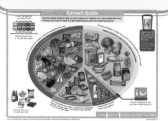

Seasonal/local foods – are these available? What do they cost?

Do the dishes in the menu meet dietary guidelines?

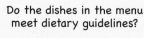

Production of dishes for a menu

Chapter 19

What do you need to know? **AC2.4**

Book link
pp168–175

- How to plan the production of a menu to a high standard and on time

LO2 Understand menu planning

Key learning

Good planning and organisation are the most important factors for the production of dishes to a high standard for a menu.

Bad planning and poor organisation lead to:

- A badly run kitchen
- Stress and wasted energy for the people who work in the kitchen and the front of house staff
- An unsuccessful business.

This is the order for the production of dishes for a menu, which is shown in detail on the following pages of this book (and also in the student textbook):

1. Planning the dishes on the menu

Book link
pp168–169

2. Producing the dishes on the menu

Book link
pp170–172

3. Serving the dishes on the menu

Book link
pp172–173

4. Preventing and dealing with waste from the menu

Book link
p173

Key terms you should try to include in your answers

Contingency – a backup plan to deal with either an emergency situation (e.g. the cooker breaks down or a special ingredient is not available) so that customer service can be restored as soon as possible; or a seasonal peak in business (e.g. Christmas) so that extra staff and equipment can be hired to cope with the increase in customers

Sequencing – also known as 'dovetailing'. This means fitting together the different stages of a production plan into a logical order. You will need to do this when you write a time plan for making two or more dishes. This is what you need to do:

1. Print a copy of each of the recipes you are going to use.

2. Highlight in the method section of each recipe, every activity you will need to do, e.g. make a dough, whisk eggs and sugar together, cut some vegetables, etc. Use a different colour highlight for each recipe to make it easier to follow.

3. Work out and show on your time plan which activity for which recipe you will do first – usually something for a recipe that needs the longest time to be completed, e.g. setting a cold mousse in the refrigerator, leaving a bread dough to rise, making some pastry and letting it rest, or cooking something for a long time.

4. Show which activity from another dish you will do next while you are waiting for the first recipe to be ready to move on to the next stage and so on, until every activity has been included.

5. When you are dovetailing the activities, remember to allow enough time for, e.g. water to boil when cooking vegetables, meat to tenderise when you are making a stew, or enough time to chop up some ingredients.

6. Remember to show when you would expect to take something out of the oven and how you would check to see that it is ready.

Plan the menu

Recipes, ingredients, preparation and cooking method for chosen dishes

Number of portions of each dish to be made

How each dish will be served / presented / garnished / decorated

Who does it? Head chef and assistant **Who needs to know?** Stock controller and every chef	**Health and safety:** High-risk foods must be safely stored	**Contingencies:** Plan alternative menus in case some ingredients are not available

Order

Ingredients and materials needed for the menu

Take in, check and store the delivery

Who does it? Stock controller and kitchen porter **Who needs to know?** Head chef	**Health and safety:** Check food delivery for quality and temperature	**Contingencies:** Buy ingredients from more than one supplier, so if one does not have an ingredient, another may have

Store

Ingredients, materials, tools and equipment tidily so they can be found and used easily

Make sure tools and equipment are clean and working properly, e.g. knives are sharpened, food processor accessories are in place, etc.

Who does it? Stock controller and kitchen porter **Who needs to know?** All chefs and kitchen workers	**Health and safety:** Food storage temperatures must be regularly checked Oldest ingredients must be used first (first in, first out)	**Contingencies:** Keep a list of companies who hire out emergency refrigerators and freezers in case one breaks down in the store room

Mise en place

Have everything (ingredients, tools and equipment) ready and in place before starting to cook

Read recipes carefully before cooking, to make sure that you know what you need to do to make a dish

Prepare ingredients, e.g. chop vegetables, prepare garnishes, weigh ingredients, cut poultry into joints

Who does it? All chefs and their assistants	**Health and safety:** Wash vegetables and fruits Store prepared foods in suitable containers at the right temperatures until they are needed	**Contingencies:** Have some extra ingredients ready in case there are more orders for a particular dish than originally planned

Sequencing

Prepare and cook dishes in a logical order

Dishes that take a long time to prepare and cook should be prepared first, e.g. bread dough needs time to rise; casseroles take a long time to cook; cold desserts need to set or freeze; stocks and sauces need time to reduce and develop flavour

Some ingredients/foods should be prepared/cooked last, e.g.: green vegetables; baked soufflés; pan fried fish

Who does it? Head chef and assistant	**Health and safety:** Use temperature probes and correct storage to keep food safe to eat Foods to be reheated for service must reach 75°C for 2 minutes

Timing

The length of time it takes for different stages of a dish to be made, e.g., how long it takes to: peel and chop vegetables; fillet fish; prepare a piece of meat or poultry for cooking; boil a pan of potatoes; bake and cool down a sponge before it can be decorated as a gateau; set a cold cheesecake, etc.

Who does it?
Head chef and assistant; all chefs

Health and safety:
Cooked foods need to be cooled as quickly as possible to prevent the growth of micro-organisms, if they are to be reheated later

Contingencies:
It may save time and be cost-effective to use some ready-made ingredients (e.g. puff pastry, pasta sauces, partially baked bread rolls) and machinery such as an electric potato peeler and large mixing machine

Cooking

Food should be cooked correctly to produce a high-quality dish
Food should be cooked with high food safety standards
As little waste as possible should be produced

Who does it?
All chefs and supervisors

Health and safety:
'Clear as you go' throughout preparation and cooking
Use temperature probes to make sure food is cooked properly

Cooling / Hot holding

Food must be kept safe and nice to eat by cooling it within 1½ hours to 5°C or below if it is to be used later
Use shallow trays or blast chillers to cool food quickly
Hot food must be kept at 63°C or above

Who does it?
All chefs and supervisors

Health and safety:
Use temperature probes to make sure food is kept at the right temperature

Completion and serving

Finishing off dishes ready for service, e.g. garnishing, decorating, serving on plates, adding accompaniments such as salad and sauces

Who does it?
All chefs and assistants

Health and safety:
Use temperature probes to check core temperatures of high-risk foods
Use serving tongs, disposable gloves and other serving equipment to prevent cross-contamination
Keep cooked and raw foods away from each other

Contingencies:
Have some extra garnishes and accompaniments available in case there are more orders than originally planned

Waste from the menu

Should be kept to a minimum
Some left-over ingredients can be used for other dishes, e.g. raw or cooked vegetables could be used in a soup; cooked meats could be used in a pie; soft fruits could be used in a fruit sauce

Who does it?
All chefs and assistants

Health and safety:
Store left-over ingredients correctly to keep them safe to eat
Get rid of food waste properly in outside bins to prevent pest infestation
Label left-over foods with the date they were made and use up as soon as possible

Contingencies:
Make an agreement with a local charity that collects left-over foods, so that food is not wasted

Activity 19.1: Put the production of the menu into order

Look at the following menu carefully with one other person.

Decide the following between you:

1. The order (sequence) in which a professional catering kitchen would produce the dishes on the menu.
2. Which ingredients the chefs would prepare during mise en place and how they would store them until they were required.
3. How the chefs would garnish/decorate each dish.

Menu

Starters

Spring vegetable soup
Served with croutons and a homemade crusty bread roll and butter

Smoked mackerel pâté and toast
Served with a salad garnish

Prawn, melon and ginger cocktail

Main courses

Slow roasted shoulder of lamb
Roasted potatoes and parsnips
Seasonal vegetables

Locally produced pork sausages in a red wine gravy
Served with creamed potatoes and peas

Deep fried haddock in a crispy batter,
Served with chips and a salad garnish

Caramelised onion, tomato and basil quiche flan
Served with jacket potato or chips, green salad and homemade coleslaw

Desserts

Lemon mousse
Served with shortbread bites

Apple pie

Baked vanilla cheesecake
Served with fruit coulis

All desserts served with either homemade ice cream, custard or whipped cream

Commodities

Chapter 20

What do you need to know? AC3.2 AC3.5

- The types of foods and ingredients (**commodities**) that are used in the Hospitality and Catering industry
- What to look for when buying and using food and ingredients (**quality points**)
- How to store commodities

Book link
pp176–184

LO3 Be able to cook dishes

Poultry

Types
Chicken
Turkey
Duck
Goose
Pigeon
Pheasant
Guinea fowl
Quail

How to store
- High-risk food
- Store at 0–5°C in refrigerator, or freeze
- To defrost frozen poultry – put on tray on bottom shelf of refrigerator (stops drips going onto other foods)
- Frozen poultry must be well wrapped to stop freezer burn
- Do not wash raw poultry before use as this spreads bacteria

What to look for when buying/using
Raw/fresh poultry should be/have:
- a fresh, pleasant smell
- moist, not wet or slimy
- springy to touch, not mushy
- pale to dark pink colour

Uses
- Goes well with many different flavours
- Used for a wide variety of dishes
- Roasted, grilled, fried, poached, stewed, braised, barbequed

Meat

Types
Pork, bacon, ham
Beef
Lamb
Mutton
Goat
Rabbit
Hare

How to store
- High-risk food
- Store at 0–5°C in refrigerator, or freeze
- To defrost frozen meat – put on tray on bottom shelf of refrigerator (stops drips going onto other foods)
- Frozen meat must be well wrapped to stop freezer burn

What to look for when buying/using
Raw/fresh meat should be/have:
- fresh, pleasant smell
- moist, not wet or slimy
- springy to touch, not mushy
- beef, lamb: bright to dark red colour
- pork, bacon, ham: pale to dark pink colour
- some visible fat under skin and between muscles (**marbling**)

Uses
- Sold as joints or cuts
- Used for a wide variety of dishes
- Roasted, grilled, fried, casseroled, stewed, braised, barbequed (depends on which part of the animal the meat comes from)

Fish

Types

Flat fish:
Plaice, sole, turbot

Round fish:
Cod, haddock, salmon, mackerel, sea bass, herring, sardine

Oily fish:
Mackerel, salmon, herring, sardine, tuna

White fish:
Cod, haddock, whiting, sea bass, bream

Seafood:
Shellfish – mussels, scallops, cockles, etc.

Crustaceans - prawns, crabs, lobsters, shrimps, etc.

What to look for when buying/using
Raw/fresh fish should be/have:

- moist, not wet or slimy
- springy to touch, not mushy
- firmly attached scales
- a fresh, pleasant smell
- bright red gills (flaps behind the eyes)
- clear, shiny eyes – not dull and sunken

Shellfish, e.g. mussels:

- mussels that are **open before cooking** are **dead and unsafe to eat**
- mussels that are **closed after cooking** are **dead and unsafe to eat**

How to store

- High-risk food
- Store at 0–5°C in refrigerator, or freeze
- Wrap well to prevent smell going into other foods
- To defrost frozen fish/seafood – put on tray on bottom shelf of refrigerator (stops drips going onto other foods)
- Frozen fish/seafood must be well wrapped to stop freezer burn

Uses

- Fish is sold whole, or as fillets, loins, cutlets
- Delicate, so only cooked for a short time
- Used for a wide variety of dishes
- Grilled, fried, stewed, baked, barbequed

Eggs

Types
Hen

Duck

Goose

Quail

What to look for when buying/using

- Shells should not be cracked
- Egg yolk should stand up in a dome shape
- Should have a fresh, pleasant smell
- Should have a thick, jelly-like egg white

How to store
High-risk food

- Store at 0–5°C in refrigerator
- Store away from other foods
- Do not wash dirty eggs until just before using them
- Always wash hands after handling raw eggs

Uses

- Used for a wide variety of sweet and savoury dishes
- Whisking – trapping air for cakes, mousses, meringue, etc.
- Setting mixtures (**coagulation** of protein), e.g. quiches, egg custard, cakes, coatings on fried food, etc.
- Binding mixtures together, e.g. burgers, fishcakes
- Glazing pastries, breads, scones
- Making mayonnaise and Hollandaise sauce (**emulsification** of oil and water)
- Adding nutrients (**enriching**) to sauces, salads, rice dishes, etc.
- Boiled, poached, scrambled, fried, baked

Dairy products

Types
Milk
Butter
Cream
Yogurt
Cheese

How to store
- High-risk foods
- Store at 0–5°C in refrigerator
- Store away from other foods
- Fresh milk can be frozen
- Whipped cream can be frozen

What to look for when buying/using
- Milk should smell fresh, not sour
- Butter should not smell sour (**rancid**)
- Buttermilk should smell fresh
- Cream should have a fresh, pleasant smell
- Soured cream (a commercial product) should have an acidic smell and flavour
- Yogurt should have a slightly acidic smell and flavour
- Cheese should not be mouldy

Uses
- Used for a wide variety of sweet and savoury dishes
- Cream: whisking to thicken double or whipping cream for piped decorations and desserts, pouring single cream to enrich desserts, soups, sauces
- Buttermilk used for scones and in sauces, drinks, cakes, desserts
- Yogurt used for desserts, cakes, drinks, sauces

Cereals

Types

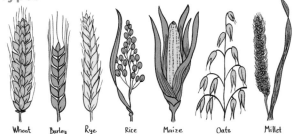

Wheat   Barley   Rye   Rice   Maize   Oats   Millet

What to look for when buying/using
- There should be no mould
- There should be no evidence of insects, e.g. maggots, weevils, moths
- Wholemeal flour should smell sweet, not sour

How to store
- Low-risk foods
- Store in a cool, dry, ventilated place in airtight containers
- Wholegrain cereals must be used by best-before date because they will go stale (rancid)

Uses
- Made into different types of flour or used as wholegrain seeds
- Wheat and rye flour used for breads, pastries, pasta, cakes, biscuits, etc.
- Maize (sweetcorn) used as a vegetable, popcorn, cornflour, corn bread, tortillas, corn oil
- Rice is a main (**staple**) food for many countries and is used in many types of sweet and savoury dishes
- Oats are used for porridge, biscuits, flapjacks, muesli, etc.

Vegetables

Types

Leaves: cabbage, lettuce, herbs, Brussels sprouts

Stems: celery, asparagus

Roots: carrots, parsnips, beetroot, swede, turnip, ginger, kohlrabi, turmeric

Bulbs: onions, garlic, leeks, spring onions, fennel

Tubers: potatoes, sweet potatoes, yam, cassava

Seeds: beans, lentils, peas

Vegetable fruits: peppers, courgettes, tomatoes, butternut squash, okra, avocados, cucumber

What to look for when buying/using

- Bright colours
- Undamaged skin
- No mould
- Smooth skin
- Not too much soil on root vegetables
- Firm, crisp texture

How to store

- Wash all vegetables before use
- Do not store dirty vegetables next to other foods
- Do not use mouldy vegetables
- Store potatoes in the dark to prevent them going green
- Potatoes that have gone green are poisonous
- Raw/dried kidney beans must be soaked in cold water for several hours then boiled for at least 15 minutes to destroy the natural poison they contain

Uses

- Used in a wide variety of dishes
- Vegetables add colour, flavour and texture
- Used as side dishes for main meals
- Used as garnishes

Fruits

Types

Stone fruits: plums, apricots, peaches, nectarines,

Berries: strawberries, raspberries, gooseberries, grapes

Currants: black, red and white currants

Citrus fruits: oranges, lemons, limes, grapefruit, tangerines, satsumas, clementines, kumquats

Hard fruits: apples, pears

Exotic fruits: melon, kiwi fruit, banana, guava, pineapple, passion fruit, pawpaw

What to look for when buying/using

- Bright colours
- Undamaged skin
- Good texture (not too soft)
- Smooth skin (except passion fruit that have wrinkled skin when ripe)

How to store

- Wash fruits before use
- Store soft fruits (berries and currants) in refrigerator
- Remove mouldy fruit to stop the mould spreading

Uses

- Used in a wide variety of dishes
- Fruits add colour, texture and flavour
- Starters for main meals
- Ingredient in many types of desserts
- Drinks – smoothies, juices, cocktails
- Garnishes and decorations
- Fruit sauces (coulis)
- Jellies – fresh pineapple, kiwi fruit and papaya will not let jelly set

Soya products

Types

Tofu (soya bean curd) – silken, firm, smoked

Tempeh – fermented soya beans

Textured Vegetable Protein (TVP), made from soya bean flour

What to look for when buying/using

- Should smell fresh
- No mould

How to store

- Use by best-before date
- When opened, store fresh tofu and tempeh in refrigerator
- Dried TVP should be stored in an airtight container in a cool cupboard

Uses

- Used in a wide variety of dishes, often in place of meat and fish
- They take up the flavours of other foods

Tofu

Tempeh

Textured Vegetable Protein (TVP)

Activity 20.1: Food safety practices when using commodities

In the **first** column of the chart below, there is a list of instructions for things you should do to keep different foods safe to eat when storing and preparing them.

For each of the foods shown after the chart, choose the correct instructions for storing and preparing them to make sure they are safe to eat. In the **second** column of the chart, put the name of each food next to the right instruction.

 Remember!
There may be more than one instruction for each food.

Here is an example to help you, e.g.: for cooked chicken, you should choose numbers: 2, 4 and 16

Instructions	Food commodities
1. Wash this food thoroughly before use	
2. Wash your hands thoroughly after handling this food	Cooked chicken
3. Do not wash this food before preparing it	
4. Store this food in the refrigerator and use it within a few days	Cooked chicken
5. Store this food in an airtight box in a cool, well-ventilated cupboard	
6. Wrap this food well and store it in the refrigerator away from other foods	
7. Store this food in the refrigerator away from other foods, to prevent smells from them passing into it	
8. Do not allow this food to touch other foods or drip on them in the refrigerator, especially cooked foods	
9. Remove this food and throw it away to stop it affecting other foods	
10. Throw this food away as it is poisonous	
11. Put this food on a tray on the bottom shelf of the refrigerator to defrost	

12. Use a blue chopping board when preparing this food	
13. Use a red chopping board when preparing this food	
14. Use a brown chopping board when preparing this food	
15. Use a green chopping board when preparing this food	
16. Use a yellow chopping board when preparing this food	Cooked chicken
17. Use a white chopping board when preparing this food	

Green potatoes

Dirty carrots

Raw chicken

Opened carton – some milk used

Raw fish

Raw minced beef

Raw eggs

Fresh salad foods

Flour – open packet

Cooked ham

Fresh cheese

Crunchy fresh bread

Raw lamb chops

Frozen prawns

Plain sponge cake

Mouldy strawberries

Frozen cooked chicken pieces

Fresh cream gateau

Chapter 21

What do you need to know? (AC3.1) (AC3.3) (AC3.4) (AC3.5)

- How different techniques are used to prepare foods
- Which cooking methods are best for different foods
- How to present dishes that people want to eat because they are creative and appetising

Book link
pp185–215

LO3 Be able to cook dishes

Key learning

For the practical part of the assessment in Unit 2, you will be asked to plan, prepare, cook and serve a variety of dishes that are:

- Suitable for a particular situation and customer needs
- Produced in a hygienic way so that the food is safe to eat
- Nutritionally balanced
- Appetising and creatively presented.

During the course, you will have had the opportunity to learn and develop a variety of skills, including:

- Menu planning
- Food preparation and cooking techniques
- Organisation and time management.

The practical part of the assessment is your opportunity to demonstrate these skills and produce and present a range of dishes that show what you are able to achieve.

⚠️ **Remember!**

When you plan your practical assessment, try to use a wide variety of food preparation techniques, cooking methods and food presentations to show the skills you have learned.

> **Study tip**
>
> This chapter gives you a summary of the techniques, cooking methods and presentation methods that you need to know about. For more detailed information about each (e.g. recipes) please refer to the student textbook, pages 185–215.

Techniques used to prepare foods (AC3.1) (AC3.5)

Measuring ingredients
Book link
p185

You should measure ingredients carefully because:

- Recipes are less likely to go wrong when you make them
- It helps the stock controller know how many ingredients to order
- It helps the kitchen to work out how many portions the recipe will make.

To measure dry ingredients, use a **digital scale** and **measuring spoons** or **measuring cups**.

To measure liquid ingredients, use a **measuring jug** and **measuring spoons** or **measuring cups**.

⚠️ **Remember!**

Set digital scales to 0:0 before adding another ingredient.

The ingredients in a measuring spoon should be level, unless the recipe says 'heaped' spoonful.

To measure liquid accurately in a measuring jug, place the jug on a level surface.

Knife/cutting skills
Book link
pp186–187

- Choose the right knife for the food you need to cut.
- Knives should be kept sharp so that they work properly.
- A blunt knife does not cut food well and is dangerous because you have to put more pressure on it to make it cut. This could make the blade slip and cause a deep cut in your hand.

Techniques – there are various techniques for cutting ingredients, e.g.:

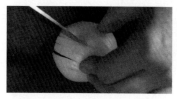

- Bridge hold for cutting an onion
- Claw grip to cut courgette, celery, or cucumber into slices
- Slicing a carrot into batons or julienne sticks

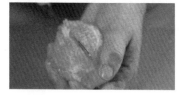

- Segmenting an orange
- Peeling vegetables with a knife or vegetable peeler
- Zesting citrus fruits with a zester or grater

Melting ingredients   Book link pp187–188

- Always use a low heat to melt fat, syrup, sugar, creamed coconut, chocolate.
- You can use a double saucepan or a heatproof bowl over simmering water (called a bain-marie).

Whisking ingredients   Book link pp188–189

- Whisking traps air in a mixture to make it light, e.g. eggs and sugar for a sponge; egg whites and sugar for a meringue; egg whites and yolk for a soufflé.
- Egg white and egg yolk proteins trap the air during whisking.

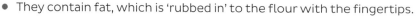
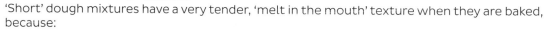

Rubbing in   Book link p190

'Short' dough mixtures have a very tender, 'melt in the mouth' texture when they are baked, because:

- They contain fat, which is 'rubbed in' to the flour with the fingertips.
- This coats the fine grains of flour with a waterproof layer of fat.
- When liquid is added to the mixture, the layers of fat only let short strands of gluten form.

Rubbing in is used to make shortbread, shortcrust pastry, scones, rock cakes and crumbles.

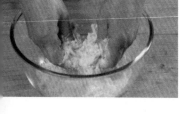

Sieving ingredients

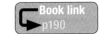
Book link p190

Ingredients are sieved to:

- Separate different sized particles of ingredients, e.g. separating raspberry seeds from the raspberry flesh to make a smooth fruit coulis sauce.
- Remove lumps from ingredients, such as flour and icing sugar.
- Trap air between flour grains when it is sieved, to make a light mixture.
- Evenly spread out a mixture of dry ingredients through a sieve, e.g. flour, plus baking powder, plus dry powdered spices or cocoa powder, for a cake mixture.
- Make a smooth soup or sauce by rubbing cooked ingredients through the sieve. This takes a lot of time, so is usually done in an electric blender instead .

Shaping ingredients

Book link p191

Ingredients can be shaped by using:

Hands, e.g.:

Making a plaited bread roll

Shaping some meat pasties

Making meat balls

Modelling sugar craft cake decoration

Tools, e.g.:

Piping bag

Pasta shaping machine

Cookie cutters

A sharp knife to shape vegetables and fruit

Blending ingredients

Book link p192

Ingredients are blended together to make them thoroughly mixed and the right texture, e.g.: cornflour is slowly blended with water or milk to stop lumps forming when making a sauce or custard.

The word 'blending' is also used to describe how different types of the same food, e.g. types of tea leaves or fruit juices, are put together to create a particular flavour. 'Juice flights' are now popular in some restaurants. These are blended fruit juices that are served with different parts of a meal to complement the flavour of the foods, similar to the way different wines are served with particular foods in a meal.

Hydrating ingredients

Book link p192

Hydrating means soaking a dried food, e.g. chickpeas, in cold water for several hours to allow it time to take up (absorb) the water (hydrate) and become ready to be cooked. Once the food has been soaked, the soaking water should be thrown away and the food should be boiled in fresh water.

Dried mushrooms being hydrated in water

Other foods will take up water or other liquids, e.g. dried fruits, lentils, nuts, dried mushrooms, noodles, dried TVP, dried milk, cereal grains, seeds, couscous and salted fish.

Soaking fresh fruits and vegetables in cold/iced water can help to refresh them if they have gone soft or wilted in hot weather.

Salad leaves in water

Cooking methods AC3.3 AC3.5

Book link
pp193–201

Foods are cooked in different ways. You should choose suitable methods of cooking for particular foods to show your skill and creativity. The chart below shows different cooking methods, how they affect the ingredients and the sensory qualities of the food, and suitable foods that can be cooked by each method.

Key terms you should try to include in your answers

Caramelise – when sugar is heated and becomes a syrup, it changes colour to golden brown and develops a toffee flavour

Coagulate – when lots of protein molecules in a food join together during cooking and change the appearance and texture of the food, e.g. make it change from a liquid to a solid

Dextrin – small groups of glucose molecules that are formed when a starchy food is cooked by dry heat, e.g. when toasting a slice of bread

Gelatinise – starch granules swell up as they are cooked in a boiling liquid and eventually burst and thicken the liquid, e.g. in a sauce

Gluten – the protein formed in wheat flour when liquid is added to it, e.g. in bread making – it gives the bread dough a stretchy texture

Palatability – what makes a food pleasing and good to eat

Starch granules – tiny particles that contain starch and are found in starchy foods, e.g. rice, flour, potatoes

Cooking methods that use liquid to cook the food

Boiling

Boiling means cooking food in water at 100°C.

Suitable foods:

Eggs, rice, pasta, vegetables such as carrots, potatoes, swede; joints of meat such as gammon (bacon/ham), beans, peas, lentils, vegetable or meat stock

What happens to the ingredients when they are cooked by this method?	What are the effects of this method of cooking on the sensory qualities of the food?	
	The appearance of the food (colour, size, shape, etc.)?	The palatability of the food (texture, aroma, flavour)?
• **Starch granules** in foods such as potatoes, rice, flour and pasta absorb water and **gelatinise** between 60°C and 100°C • Protein **coagulates** (goes solid), e.g. egg white protein coagulates at 60°C and egg yolk at 70°C • Fat will melt • Stocks and sauces reduce in volume as water evaporates	• Pasta, rice, beans and lentils swell up as their starch granules absorb the boiling water • Green vegetables turn bright green for a few minutes, then gradually become a dark olive green if overcooked • Red/purple fruits and vegetables are affected by acids (makes them turn a brighter red/purple) and alkalis such as bicarbonate of soda, which makes them turn blue • Egg white changes from clear to white and the yolk becomes a lighter yellow as the protein coagulates • Meat/poultry shrink in size as protein coagulates	• Pasta, rice, peas, beans and lentils become soft as they absorb the water • Vegetables become soft and tender. They may become mushy and break up if they are boiled for too long • Meat will become tender, but will dry out if boiled for too long because the protein coagulates too much and squeezes out the moisture it held • The flavour of some vegetables gets stronger, e.g. carrots become sweeter • Some flavour from meat will go into the water, but if the water is used to make gravy or stock, the flavour will be saved • The flavour of stock and sauces will get stronger as the water evaporates

Braising

Braising means sealing in hot oil, then cooking slowly in a covered dish with a little liquid.

Suitable foods:

Meat, poultry, tagines, vegetables, e.g. carrots, fennel, red cabbage

What happens to the ingredients when they are cooked by this method?	What are the effects of this method of cooking on the sensory qualities of the food?	
	The appearance of the food (colour, size, shape, etc.)?	The palatability of the food (texture, aroma, flavour)?
• Starch granules absorb water and gelatinise • Protein coagulates • Meat tenderises • Vegetables tenderise • Fat will melt	• The colour of red meat becomes brown • Meat/poultry shrink in size as protein coagulates • Red cabbage becomes a deep red/purple colour • Sauces become glossy (shiny)	• Meat, poultry and vegetables become tender • Food cooks slowly and absorbs flavours from stock, vegetables, herbs and spices that are added to it

Poaching

Poaching means cooking food in a shallow pan of water or wine at just under boiling point, with only a few bubbles showing.

Suitable foods:

Chicken, fish, eggs, fruit, e.g. pears

What happens to the ingredients when they are cooked by this method?	What are the effects of this method of cooking on the sensory qualities of the food?	
	The appearance of the food (colour, size, shape, etc.)?	The palatability of the food (texture, aroma, flavour)?
• Protein coagulates • Fruit softens	• Egg white changes from clear to white and the yolk becomes a lighter yellow as the protein coagulates • Fish shrinks slightly and separates into flakes of muscle as the protein coagulates	• Fish and poultry become tender • Fish is less likely to be overcooked because the temperature of the water is just under boiling point and it is easy to see when the protein has coagulated • Some flavour from poultry and fish will go into the water, but if the water is used to make gravy or stock, the flavour will be saved • The time needed to poach fruit, e.g. pears in wine and spices, allows the flavours from the poaching liquid to be absorbed by the fruit

Simmering

Simmering means cooking food in a liquid just below boiling point, so that it bubbles gently.

Suitable foods:

Vegetables, soups, stews, fruit, e.g. apples, meat sauces, e.g. Bolognese sauce, curries, chowders (chunky soup)

What happens to the ingredients when they are cooked by this method?	What are the effects of this method of cooking on the sensory qualities of the food?	
	The appearance of the food (colour, size, shape, etc.)?	The palatability of the food (texture, aroma, flavour)?
• Starch granules absorb water and gelatinise • Protein coagulates • Fat will melt • Stock reduces in volume as water evaporates • Fruit softens	• Colours of ingredients become stronger • Volume (the amount of liquid) may reduce	• Meat and poultry become tender • Vegetables become tender • Food cooks slowly and absorbs flavours from stock, vegetables, herbs and spices

Steaming

Steaming means cooking food in the steam rising from a pan of boiling water beneath.

Suitable foods:

Green vegetables, e.g. broccoli, cabbage, spinach, kale, Brussels sprouts; white fish; dim sum dumplings; sponge puddings; rice

What happens to the ingredients when they are cooked by this method?	What are the effects of this method of cooking on the sensory qualities of the food?	
	The appearance of the food (colour, size, shape, etc.)?	The palatability of the food (texture, aroma, flavour)?
• Starch granules absorb water and gelatinise • Protein coagulates • Fat will melt • Fruit and vegetables soften	• Green vegetables turn bright green for a few minutes, then gradually become a dark olive green if overcooked • Fish shrinks slightly and separates into flakes of muscle as the protein coagulates • Sponge puddings rise and set, but do not develop a golden crust because the starch they contain does not turn to **dextrin** in moist heat   • Dim sums swell as the starch granules in the flour gelatinise, and the filling coagulates and sets • Rice grains swell as the starch granules they contain gelatinise	• Food cooks gently and is unlikely to be overcooked • Foods become tender and develop a soft, moist texture that is easy to digest

Stewing

Stewing means cooking food by simmering it gently in a covered pot in the oven, on the hob or in a slow cooker.

Suitable foods:

Meat, poultry, sausages, casseroles, fruit, e.g. apples, plums, rhubarb

What happens to the ingredients when they are cooked by this method?	What are the effects of this method of cooking on the sensory qualities of the food?	
	The appearance of the food (colour, size, shape, etc.)?	The palatability of the food (texture, aroma, flavour)?
• Starch granules absorb water and gelatinise • Protein coagulates • Meat becomes tender • Fat will melt • Fruit and vegetables soften	• Colours of ingredients become stronger • Volume may reduce as water evaporates • Glossy sauce develops • Colour of red meat becomes brown • Meat/poultry shrink in size as protein coagulates • Fruit colours become stronger • Red/purple fruits and vegetables are affected by acids (makes them a brighter red/purple) and alkalis such as bicarbonate of soda, which makes them turn blue 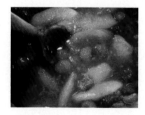	• Same as for braising

Cooking methods that use dry heat to cook the food

Baking

Baking means cooking foods in a hot oven.

Suitable foods:

Cakes, breads, biscuits, cookies, scones, pastries, potatoes, pizzas, desserts

What happens to the ingredients when they are cooked by this method?	What are the effects of this method of cooking on the sensory qualities of the food?	
	The appearance of the food (colour, size, shape, etc.)?	The palatability of the food (texture, aroma, flavour)?
<ul><li>Gases from raising agents expand with the heat and make mixtures rise</li><li>Protein coagulates</li><li>Added sugars melt and form a syrup that softens the **gluten**</li><li>Added sugars eventually **caramelise**</li><li>Fat will melt</li><li>Starch granules absorb water and/or melted fat</li><li>Starch granules absorb moisture, swell and gelatinise</li><li>Alcohol produced by yeast in bread doughs evaporates in the heat of the oven</li><li>Yeast is killed by the heat</li><li>Gluten, egg proteins and starch set and form a framework around the gas bubbles inside baked products</li></ul>	<ul><li>Baked foods containing raising agents rise and expand before setting in the heat of the oven</li></ul>  <ul><li>Starch in the outside crust of baked goods turns to dextrin and turns a golden-brown colour</li><li>Caramelised sugars add golden brown colour</li></ul>	<ul><li>Risen food sets and develops a tender, open/crumbly/spongy texture inside</li></ul> <ul><li>A crust develops on the outside</li><li>Caramelised sugars add flavour</li></ul>

Roasting

Roasting means cooking food in some fat or oil in the oven.

Suitable foods:

Meat and poultry joints; root vegetables; some fruits, e.g. plums; nuts

What happens to the ingredients when they are cooked by this method?	What are the effects of this method of cooking on the sensory qualities of the food?	
	The appearance of the food (colour, size, shape, etc.)?	The palatability of the food (texture, aroma, flavour)?
<ul><li>Starch absorbs oil and softens</li><li>Natural sugars in vegetables and fruit caramelise</li><li>Protein coagulates</li><li>Fruit and vegetables soften</li></ul>	<ul><li>Red meat turns brown; poultry turns creamy/white colour</li><li>Onions, parsnips, carrots become golden brown due to caramelisation of sugars</li><li>Colours of vegetables get stronger</li><li>Vegetables shrink as water evaporates from them</li><li>Skin on poultry and fat on meat, e.g. pork, becomes golden brown</li></ul><ul><li>Juices from meat and poultry are squeezed out and develop into a golden-brown glaze in the roasting pan</li></ul><ul><li>Meat/poultry shrink in size as protein coagulates</li></ul>	<ul><li>Vegetables/fruits tenderise inside and develop a crisp outer texture</li></ul> <ul><li>Juices from meat and poultry are squeezed out and develop flavour on the surface</li><li>Skin/fat on outside of joints of meat/poultry become crisp</li><li>Overcooking causes meat/poultry to dry out and become difficult to digest</li></ul>

Grilling/barbequing

Grilling/barbequing means cooking foods by intense radiant heat on a metal grid or grill rack, underneath a heated grill element in a cooker **or** above the glowing charcoal/flames in a barbeque.

Suitable foods:

Meat and poultry joints, oily fish, sausages, burgers, toppings for gratin dishes (cheese sauce), halloumi cheese, tomatoes, sweetcorn cobs

What happens to the ingredients when they are cooked by this method?	What are the effects of this method of cooking on the sensory qualities of the food?	
	The appearance of the food (colour, size, shape, etc.)?	The palatability of the food (texture, aroma, flavour)?
• Protein coagulates rapidly • Fat melts and drains away from the food • Starch turns to dextrin • Sugars caramelise	• Meat/poultry will shrink rapidly due to protein coagulating • Fat melts and drains out • Surface of meat/poultry develops a golden-brown colour	• Juices from meat and poultry are squeezed out and develop flavour on the surface • If cooked too rapidly, meat and poultry can become dry and chewy due to protein coagulating and squeezing out water • Flavour gets stronger as water evaporates

Toasting

Toasting means cooking starch-based foods with dry heat from a grill or flame.

Suitable foods:

Bread, buns, crumpets and other starch-based products, nuts, seeds

What happens to the ingredients when they are cooked by this method?	What are the effects of this method of cooking on the sensory qualities of the food?	
	The appearance of the food (colour, size, shape, etc.)?	The palatability of the food (texture, aroma, flavour)?
• Starch turns to dextrin	• Food develops a golden-brown crust	• Flavour gets stronger • Crust adds texture to the food

Dry frying

Dry frying means cooking food that naturally contains oil or fat in a frying pan without adding oil.

Suitable foods:

Minced meat, e.g. beef, lamb, pork; nuts, seeds, whole spices

What happens to the ingredients when they are cooked by this method?	What are the effects of this method of cooking on the sensory qualities of the food?	
	The appearance of the food (colour, size, shape, etc.)?	The palatability of the food (texture, aroma, flavour)?
• Starch changes to dextrin • Fat will melt; natural oils will soften • Protein will coagulate	• Food develops a golden-brown colour • The oils in nuts and seeds melt and are released • Meat changes to a brown colour and fat and juices are released from it	• Flavour gets stronger • Oils are released and add texture and flavour • Fat in meat melts and drains out of it • Proteins in meat coagulate and squeeze out juices from the meat, and add to its flavour

Cooking methods that use oil to cook the food

Sautéing

Sautéing means frying food gently in a little oil in order to soften the food and develop flavour.

Suitable foods:

Onions, leeks, peppers, meat/poultry and vegetables used as a base for soups and stews, celery, carrot, butternut squash, sweet potato, courgette

What happens to the ingredients when they are cooked by this method?	What are the effects of this method of cooking on the sensory qualities of the food?	
	The appearance of the food (colour, size, shape, etc.)?	The palatability of the food (texture, aroma, flavour)?
• Natural sugars caramelise • Starch granules absorb oil and swell • Protein coagulates	• Onions, parsnips, carrots become golden brown due to caramelisation • Red meat turns brown; poultry turns creamy/white colour • Meat/poultry shrink in size as protein coagulates	• Caramelised vegetables taste sweeter • Flavour gets stronger as water evaporates • As meat and poultry cook, protein coagulates and shrinks and juices are squeezed out and form flavour on the surface

Shallow frying (pan frying)

Shallow frying (pan frying) means frying food in a shallow frying pan in a little oil.

Suitable foods:

Eggs, fish (white or oily), bacon, burgers, sausages, meat cuts such as chops, cutlets, and steaks, pancakes, flat breads, onions, potato slices, fishcakes, potato cakes, rissoles, bananas

What happens to the ingredients when they are cooked by this method?	What are the effects of this method of cooking on the sensory qualities of the food?	
	The appearance of the food (colour, size, shape, etc.)?	The palatability of the food (texture, aroma, flavour)?
• Starch granules absorb oil and soften • Protein coagulates • Fat will melt • Cell structure of fruit and vegetables softens • Coatings such as egg and breadcrumbs (used for fish, chicken breast, fishcakes, potato cakes), will protect the food inside from drying out and overcooking as the egg protein coagulates and seals the food from the intense heat of frying	• Egg white changes from clear to white and the yolk becomes a lighter yellow as the protein coagulates • Fish shrinks slightly and separates into flakes of muscle as the protein coagulates 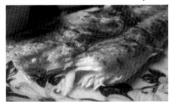 • Onions, parsnips, carrots become golden brown due to caramelisation • Red meat turns brown; poultry turns creamy/white colour • Meat/poultry shrink in size as protein coagulates	• Foods develop a crispy texture on the outside, especially if the food is coated with, e.g. egg and breadcrumbs  • Some vegetables will caramelise and become sweeter • Vegetables/fruits will soften as the starch and cell walls they contain soften • As meat and poultry cook, protein coagulates and shrinks, and juices are squeezed out and form flavour on the surface

147

Stir frying

Stir frying means frying food for a short time in a wok at a high temperature, using very little oil and stirring all the time.

Suitable foods:

Finely cut vegetables and other foods, e.g. peppers, onion, mushrooms, courgettes, pak choi, spring onions, bean sprouts, mange tout peas, bamboo shoots, root ginger, seafood, fish, meat, poultry, nuts, tofu

What happens to the ingredients when they are cooked by this method?	What are the effects of this method of cooking on the sensory qualities of the food?	
	The appearance of the food (colour, size, shape, etc.)?	The palatability of the food (texture, aroma, flavour)?
• Starch granules absorb oil and soften • Protein coagulates • Fruit and vegetables soften	• Colours of vegetables get stronger • Vegetables shrink as water evaporates from them • Meat /poultry/seafood shrink in size as protein coagulates	• Quickness of stir frying helps to preserve the flavours of the vegetables • Vegetables soften a little but stay quite crisp • Meat /poultry/fish cook quickly so must be cut into small pieces in order to be tender and cooked right through

Microwaving

Microwaving means cooking food by electromagnetic waves called microwaves in a microwave oven.

Suitable foods:

Sauces, cake and sponge pudding mixtures, scrambled eggs, vegetables, fruits, fish, soups, melting chocolate and butter

What happens to the ingredients when they are cooked by this method?	What are the effects of this method of cooking on the sensory qualities of the food?	
	The appearance of the food (colour, size, shape, etc.)?	The palatability of the food (texture, aroma, flavour)?
• Water molecules vibrate and transfer heat energy to the food • Protein coagulates • Fat melts • Sugar will caramelise and burn easily • Starch will gelatinise in the presence of moisture	• Cakes, sponge puddings, meat, and other foods do not develop much colour • Juices and water from meat will leak out as the protein coagulates and squeezes them out	• Meat will not develop flavours on the outside as it does in frying, roasting or grilling • Overcooking may result in sugars or chocolate burning easily

Induction cooking

Induction cooking is a method of cooking where heat energy is transferred quickly to a pan through a specially designed ceramic cooking surface, over an induction coil that creates a magnetic current. Pans that are used on induction hobs must be magnetic, e.g. cast iron, magnetic stainless steel or steel.

What happens to the ingredients when they are cooked by this method?	What are the effects of this method of cooking on the sensory qualities of the food?	
	The appearance of the food (colour, size, shape, etc.)?	The palatability of the food (texture, aroma, flavour)?
• Same as for other methods of cooking carried out on the hob	• Same as for other methods of cooking carried out on the hob	• Same as for other methods of cooking carried out on the hob

Important temperatures in catering you should know and use in your practical assessment production plan

Book link pp201–202

Food production stage:	Food delivery to kitchen
Safe temperatures:	Refrigerated foods: **0°C to 5°C**
	Frozen foods: **–22°C to –18°C**
Notes:	If a higher temperature, do not accept the food.

Food production stage:	Food storage – high-risk foods (milk, butter, cream, yogurt, cheese, meat, meat products, fish, seafood, poultry)
Safe temperatures:	Refrigerated / cold store foods: **0°C to 5°C** (England and Northern Ireland) **up to 8°C** (Wales and Scotland)
	Frozen foods: **–22° to –18°C**
Notes:	Check refrigerator and freezer temperatures every day.

Food production stage:	Defrosting frozen meat, poultry, fish or seafood
Safe temperatures:	**0°C to 5°C**
Notes:	Defrost on a tray (to prevent drips) in the refrigerator or cold store.

Food production stage:	Cooking high-risk foods
Safe temperatures:	Core temperature: **minimum 70°C for 2 minutes** to destroy any pathogenic (harmful) bacteria
Notes:	Use a food probe that has been checked (calibrated) for accuracy by placing it in ice to check that it reads 0°C or just under; then placing it in boiling water to check that it reads 100°C.

Food production stage:	Cooling cooked foods
Safe temperatures:	The food should reach **5°C or cooler within 1½ hours** to prevent the growth and multiplication of bacteria
Notes:	Food will cool down quickly in a blast chiller or well-ventilated room away from the heat of the kitchen.
	Foods such as cooked rice can be cooled quickly by rinsing in very cold water.
	Foods such as meat sauces can be poured into large shallow trays. The large surface area helps them to cool quickly.

Food production stage:	Blanching
	Food is blanched to soften it, or to partially cook it, or to remove something from it e.g.:
	• Nuts can be blanched to remove their skins, e.g. almonds, hazelnuts
	• Vegetables, such as fresh peas and beans, are blanched to destroy natural chemicals called enzymes, which would cause vitamin, colour, texture and flavour changes to the vegetables during storage
Safe temperatures:	Vegetables can be blanched in boiling **(100°C)** water for a few minutes.
	They are then rapidly cooled (refreshed) in iced water and chilled until needed later.
	They can be reheated quickly, ready for service.
	Potato chips/fries can be blanched in hot oil **(130°C)** to cook the inside of the potato. They are then drained, and later fried in hotter oil **(190°C)** to make the outside really crisp.
Notes:	Blanching destroys enzymes and bacteria on the surface of vegetables and keeps their bright colour, texture and vitamin content.

149

Food production stage:	Reheating cooked and chilled foods
Safe temperatures:	Core temperature: **minimum 70°C for 2 minutes** in England, Wales and Northern Ireland; **minimum of 82°C** in Scotland
Notes:	Cooked foods should only be reheated **once** to prevent the growth and multiplication of bacteria.

Food production stage:	Hot holding – keeping cooked food hot for service
Safe temperatures:	**Minimum 63°C**
Notes:	This temperature prevents the growth and multiplication of bacteria.

Food production stage:	Cold holding / chilled foods displayed for service
Safe temperatures:	**0°C to 5°C**
Notes:	This temperature prevents the growth and multiplication of bacteria.

Activity 21.1: Which is the correct temperature?

Match the correct temperature information to the correct food production stage.

Cooking high-risk foods

0 to 5°C

Core temperature: minimum 70°C for 2 minutes

Core temperature: minimum 70°C for 2 minutes (England, Wales and Northern Ireland). In Scotland the core temperature must be a minimum of 82°C.

Cooling cooked foods

Hot holding – keeping cooked food hot for service

Refrigerated foods should be: 0 to 5°C
Frozen foods should be: –22 to –18°C

Checking the temperature of high-risk foods when they are delivered to the kitchen

Core temperature: minimum 63°C

Cold holding /chilled foods displayed for service

0 to 5°C

Storing high-risk foods in a refrigerator, cold store or freezer

Defrosting frozen meat, poultry, fish and seafood

The food should reach 5°C or cooler within 1½ hours

Refrigerated /cold-store foods should be:
0 to 5°C (England and Northern Ireland)
Up to 8°C in Wales and Scotland
Frozen foods should be: –22 to –18°C

Reheating cooked and chilled foods

Presentation methods AC3.4 AC3.5

Book link
pp157–161

General advice on presenting food:

1. **Have all the ingredients ready and cooked before starting to put the food on the plate.**
2. **Choose a suitable plate / serving platter:**
   - Not too big.
   - Not too small.
   - White or black plates will show off the colours of the food.
   - Plates and platters are made from a variety of materials, e.g. wood, ceramic/china, slate, stone (e.g. granite), stainless steel, banana leaves, bamboo stems, etc.
   - If the food is hot, the plate should be warmed.
   - Cold food should be served on a cold plate.
   - Wipe the edges of the plate with a clean cloth or fresh piece of kitchen paper to remove food drips and spills before serving.

> **Remember!**
> The first sense that people use when choosing and enjoying their food is sight.
>
> Good presentation of a dish will make people want to choose it and they will enjoy eating it.
>
> There are no set rules about how food should be presented – this is down to you. Be creative!

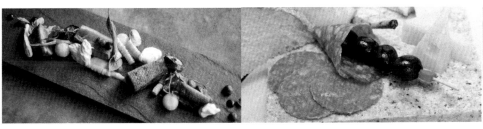

3. **Place the ingredients on the plate/platter:**
   - Not too much – the plate should be a frame around the food.
   - Do not have food hanging over the edges of the plate.
   - Have one ingredient as the focal point of the plate, e.g. the protein / main food (e.g. meat, fish or vegetarian main). This is often placed to one side of the dish, rather than directly in the centre, with the rest of the foods around it like this:
   - Foods such as potatoes and meat balls, are often served in odd numbers (e.g. 3, 5, or 7) as it makes it look like there is more food on the plate.

4. **Be creative:**
   - Make use of the natural colours and shapes of foods.
   - Combine different textures, e.g. smooth sauces with crunchy chopped nuts; crispy vegetables and soft purees.
   - Decorate plates creatively with sauces:

– Use caramelised sugar to make decorations:

– Make chocolate decorations, e.g. chocolate leaves, swirls, squares, etc.
– Chocolate shapes can be drizzled or piped onto non-stick silicone baking paper and allowed to cool and set, then lifted off and used as decorations. Keep shapes cool until used.
– Spread melted chocolate onto non-stick silicone baking paper and allow it to cool and set at room temperature, then cut out shapes, e.g. squares or triangles, using a sharp knife or metal cutter. Keep shapes cool until used.
– Dip fresh fruits into melted chocolate and allow to set.

5. Use garnishes and decorations

– Use garnishes and decorations that complement the other ingredients and add flavour and texture to the meal – do not use too many.

– Place the garnishes and decorations carefully on the plate to add to the creativity of the meal.
– Flowers from these plants are edible:

Basil, borage, calendula (marigold), chervil, chives, lavender, nasturtium, pansy, rose, sage. Any flowers that are used for food must be clean and **must not** have been sprayed with pesticides, fertilisers, or be contaminated with urine or faeces from animals.

There are various tools that are designed for serving food creatively, including:

Silicon plating wedge

Precision spoon

Plastic squeeze bottle

Fine tweezers

Ring mould

Portion control

Portion control means serving a portion of food that is always the same size each time.

The number of portions that a recipe makes is usually called its **yield**, e.g. a large cheesecake may yield sixteen portions.

Portion control is essential to make sure that a catering business makes a profit. If just a small amount of extra food is regularly given to customers when they are served, over a period of time the business will struggle to make a profit and may even lose money.

The amount of food that is given in a portion to customers will depend on:

- The type of customer – do they need large portions? Are they builders working on a nearby building site; or are they elderly people who may have smaller appetites?
- The type of business – e.g. roadside cafes that tend to sell 'hearty' (larger) portions compared with a fine dining restaurant where portions tend to be smaller
- How much the food costs the restaurant to buy
- The quality of the food – better-quality food tends to have less waste and gives more portions
- The knowledge of the food buyer and the chef about what to buy and the number of portion sizes needed and expected to be made from different recipes.

How to make sure that portion sizes are controlled

- Train the kitchen staff to use the correct serving equipment to make sure sizes are always the same.
- Make sure that each recipe clearly shows how many portions it will yield.
- Use portion control equipment that is designed to serve a fixed amount of food, e.g.:

In this picture of a meal of chicken casserole and vegetables, the portion size is too large so the plate is overloaded, and it would be difficult to pick up and serve as the food comes right to the edge of the plate. It also looks messy, which spoils the presentation.

Serving scoop for mashed vegetables, ice cream

Scoops to serve chips/fries

Healthy food-portion controller

Double-sided cake marker – each side gives a different number of portions

Activity 21.2: Making meals look appealing to patients in hospital

Look at the dinner menu for a hospital ward where people are recovering from operations.

Suggest some ways in which the chefs can present the dishes creatively so that the patients want to eat them:

Starter

Cream of mushroom soup with brown bread roll

OR

Hummus and crackers

Main course

Fish pie topped with mashed potatoes and served with green beans

OR

Meatballs in tomato sauce with spaghetti and served with green beans

OR

Cauliflower cheese served with peas and carrots

Dessert

Apple crumble and custard

OR

Cheddar cheese and biscuits

Chapter 22

Assessment of Unit 2 : Preparing for the Controlled Assessment Task (CAT)

What do you need to know?

Book link
pp256–280

- How you will be assessed in Unit 2 of the course
- Useful hints and tips to help you do your best in the Unit 2 assessment

Key learning

For Unit 2, you will be assessed in the following way:

- You will be given a Learner Assignment Brief (LAB), which describes a fictional (imaginary – not real) hospitality and catering business or scenario (situation) that you will be asked to write about and plan dishes for, to meet the needs of a target group of customers.

- There are three tasks that you have to do for the assessment – two are written and one is practical, and the Assessment Criteria (AC) use command words to tell you what you have to do for each.

- The assessment is called a Controlled Assessment Task (CAT), which means that it is supervised at each stage and marked by your teacher at school. At the end, it is checked (moderated) by the examination board to make sure that you have been given the right mark for the work you have done.

- There are nine stages that you have to complete: The last stage (Task 3) is a practical assessment, where you prepare, cook and present the dishes you have planned for the target group in the LAB, in a set amount of time (around 2 to 3 hours – your teacher will tell you exactly how much time you have). This gives you the chance to showcase your practical skills.

> 1. Carefully read the LAB

> 2. Write down the key words and key hospitality and catering information in the LAB, e.g. target group of customers, type of venue, etc.

> 3. TASK 1: Write about nutrition for the target group in the LAB

> 4. TASK 1: Write about menu planning for the target group in the LAB

> 5. Write about your ideas for some dishes that would be suitable for the target group in the LAB

> 6. Choose dishes you will make for the target group in the LAB in your practical assessment

> 7. TASK 2: Write about the factors you have considered when planning your chosen dishes for the target group in the LAB

> 8. TASK 2: Write a production plan for your chosen dishes

> 9. TASK 3: Prepare, cook and present your dishes for the target group in the LAB and take photographs of the results

Study tip

Before you start your assessment:

- **Read through the LAB** very carefully and several times.
- **Highlight key words.** Key words could be, for example, the type of place the brief has described, the type of customers, any special needs the customers have.
- **Understand what the LAB is asking** you to do to complete the tasks – check with your teacher if you are not sure what you have to do.
- Make sure you have **class notes or teacher's notes.** Your teacher will check these before the assessment starts.
- Have a copy of the LOs, AC, performance bands chart and mark record sheet, so you can see how many marks each part of the assessment is worth. **Your teacher should give you these before you read the LAB.**

In order to give you some guidance about what you have to do for the assessment, we are going to show each stage of an example Learner Assignment Brief (LAB), starting here:

Stage 1
Carefully read the LAB

Stage 2
Write down the key words and key hospitality and catering information in the LAB, e.g. target group of customers, type of venue, etc.

(In the example LAB, these have been highlighted for you.)

Example Learner Assignment Brief

Here you can see what the example LAB is asking you to do:

Ryeholt is a medium-sized town with a multicultural population of mixed ages. Ryeholt Sports Centre in the town has recently been re-opened after a major renovation and refit. The new management of the sports centre want to promote healthy lifestyles through the activities they offer and the food they sell in their cafe. They also want the centre to actively promote and support environmental sustainability by using solar and wind energy, recycling waste packaging and materials, reducing food and water waste and limiting their use of single-use plastics.

A new catering manager, three experienced chefs and six assistants to work in the back and front of house have been employed for the cafe.

The management want to encourage primary schoolchildren (5 to 12 years old) and teenagers (from 13 to 19 years old) to make healthy and sustainable eating choices. They are developing lunch menus for these two age groups.

Your task is to suggest four dishes for the lunch menu that would appeal to primary schoolchildren and teenagers. At least two dishes should be main courses; the other two can be starters or desserts or one of each. The dishes should demonstrate at least three food preparation skills and three cooking methods. To make sure that the dishes can be prepared and cooked with the facilities and time available, you have been asked to produce a production plan for two of the dishes and then prepare and cook them.

You now need to look at the Assessment Criteria to see what you need to put in your written work for Tasks 1 and 2 and how you could set it out.

You need to know:

- What the performance descriptors (PD) mean in each performance band
- Details of each AC and what you need to do to for each one to achieve your best level
- Different ways in which you could present your work.

Performance descriptors are the words used in the AC that explain what a student must be able to do to reach the standard required to be awarded either a level 1 or 2 pass, a level 2 merit or a level 2 distinction. They are set out in the table on the following page. They range from **red** colour-coded descriptors, where students give more detailed information, with examples and explanations, to **green** colour-coded descriptors where students give only basic information, with few examples or explanations.

Performance descriptors	What does it mean? What can the student do?
In-depth	Write about all the major points, giving detailed and thorough explanations and examples that demonstrate their knowledge and understanding.
Independently	Work on their own, without help.
Credible	Back up / justify something they have written by including evidence, e.g. a book reference, an interview, the results of a survey, etc.
Clear/clearly	Write in a way that is easy to understand and keeps to the point of the topic. It covers most of the main information.
Compare	Identify how things are similar to and different from each other.
Describe clearly	Write about the features and characteristics of a topic, place, activity, item or person, in a clear and detailed way.
Explain	Write about something in a clear way, giving the purpose of it, or reasons for it. Use examples to illustrate the answer, to show that they understand what they are writing about.
A range	Give a variety of examples or information, but not everything.
Some	Give only a small amount of information, which means they can only have a few marks.
Outline	Set out the main information as a simple list or sentence, without giving details or explaining it to show their understanding.
Limited range	The answer given only covers limited parts of the Assessment Criteria.
Describe	Write about the features and characteristics of a topic, place, activity, item or person in a simple way without much detail.

Examples of performance descriptors

To show you what to look for and see how to progress in the performance band chart, some performance descriptors (PD) for AC1.2 have been given here as an example. They are highlighted and colour-coded in the chart below to match the previous chart:

Learning Outcome	Assessment Criteria	Level 1 Pass PD	Level 2 Pass PD	Level 2 Merit PD	Level 2 Distinction PD
LO1 Understand the importance of nutrition in planning menus	AC1.2 Compare nutritional needs of specific groups	Outlines nutritional needs of two specific groups. Comparison may be implied.	Compares nutritional needs of two specific groups giving some reasons for similarities and differences.	Compares nutritional needs of two specific groups giving clear reasons for similarity and differences.	Compares nutritional needs of two specific groups giving clear and in-depth reasons for similarity and differences.

Activity 22.1: Find the performance descriptors

Highlight and **colour code** the performance descriptors for all the Assessment Criteria in LO1, LO2 and LO3 on the performance bands chart you have been given by your teacher. This will help you identify and understand what you need to do to achieve your best result in the Unit 2 Assessment.

Stage 3

TASK 1: Write about nutrition for the target groups in the LAB

How to present your written work for this part of Task 1

For the first part of Task 1 (LO1, AC1.1), you need to write about:

- The jobs that different nutrients do in the body.

You can display your written work for this part of Task 1 in a number of different styles, e.g.:

- A chart/table
- A poster
- A leaflet
- A PowerPoint presentation
- A talk/discussion, which has video evidence.

 Remember!

When you write about nutrients, you must link the information to the needs of children and teenagers to show that you understand what the LAB is asking you to do.

Here are two examples of how you can present your written work on nutrition for different groups of people:

1. A chart or table:

NB If a few more points are added to this poster it could be awarded a Level 2 pass.

Children 5–12 years old	Which nutrients they need What jobs they do in the body Which foods are they found in *(Just a few examples are given here – you would need to add more)*	Teenagers 13–19 years old

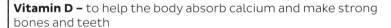

Protein – for body growth and development, which is rapid during childhood and in teenagers

Foods that contain protein:

Meat, poultry, fish, eggs, milk, cheese, yogurt, beans, lentils, peas, seeds

Vitamin D – to help the body absorb calcium and make strong bones and teeth

Foods that contain vitamin D:

Oily fish e.g. mackerel, sardines; butter, eggs, vegetable fat spreads (added by law), meat

Most vitamin D is made in the body by the action of sunlight on the skin

Iron – this is needed to make haemoglobin in red blood cells to pick up and carry oxygen to all body cells to release energy

Foods that contain iron:

Red meat, liver, wholemeal bread, green leafy vegetables, egg yolk, dried apricots, lentil, cocoa, fortified breakfast cereals

2. A poster:
NB If a few more points are added to this poster it could be awarded a Level 1 pass.

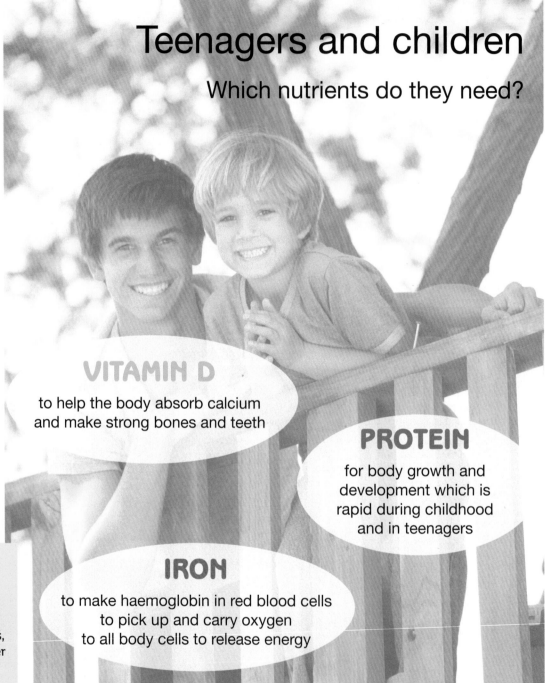

Teenagers and children

Which nutrients do they need?

(Just a few examples are given here – you would need to add more)

VITAMIN D
to help the body absorb calcium and make strong bones and teeth

PROTEIN
for body growth and development which is rapid during childhood and in teenagers

IRON
to make haemoglobin in red blood cells to pick up and carry oxygen to all body cells to release energy

⚠ *Remember!*
To get good marks, you must write about a wide range of nutrients (protein, fat, carbohydrate, vitamins, minerals and also water and dietary fibre).

For the second part of Task 1, (AC1.2) you need to compare the nutrient needs for different groups of people (in the example LAB these are children aged 5–12 years and teenagers aged 13–19 years old).

On the next page are some example answers (with comments from the assessor in the boxes) to help you see how much detail is needed in order to gain good marks.

Example answers that would be awarded a Level 1 Pass (AC1.2)

Children need all the nutrients, especially protein, because they are growing and very active. Teenagers also grow very fast, so need all the nutrients, too.

Children need to grow strong bones so they will need minerals like calcium, and teenagers need more minerals because they might grow very tall.

Children and teenagers both need carbohydrate for energy.

> ⚠ *Remember!*
>
> When you present this work, it should be clearly set out and easy to follow and read. You could use diagrams to help illustrate and explain what you are writing about.

Only a brief and basic outline given for nutritional needs of both groups.

A very brief comparison of energy needs between the two groups, but no detail has been given; e.g. children would need more energy because they are growing and very active, and teenagers need plenty of energy for rapid growth spurts, the demands of school work and an increasingly active social life. Information about the need to limit children's sugar intake could have been given here.

Information about the need to limit children's salt intake could have been given here as well as the need to encourage children to try new foods and other (non-salt) flavours.

A brief comparison about bone development but few details to show knowledge and understanding.

No information about vitamin C and iron intake has been given.

No information about water and dietary fibre intake has been given.

Example answers that would be awarded a Level 2 Merit (AC1.2)

Children and teenagers are growing and developing quickly, therefore they need all of the nutrients to allow this to happen properly. However, there are some nutrients that they particularly need at this stage of their lives. As well as growing, some children and teenagers are very physically active, which means they need lots of protein from plants and animal foods and energy from carbohydrates to help them cope with the extra demands of physical activity. They should also follow the Eatwell Guide to make sure that they develop a taste for trying and eating a variety of fresh foods, which will give them plenty of different nutrients.

Clear and well thought out comparison of general nutritional needs for both groups, with reference to the Eatwell Guide. Comparison clearly highlights similarities and differences between the needs of the body in both age groups.

Both children and teenagers need carbohydrate and fat for energy, but should limit the amount of sugar they have in their diet. This is because excess sugar can lead to weight gain and tooth decay in both age groups. Children may also prefer to eat sweet foods, which may be difficult to stop and lead to health problems such as obesity and heart disease as they get older. Teenagers may spend their dinner money on buying sweets and sweet drinks rather than eating a meal at school. The same applies to salt, because many snack foods and takeaways have a lot of salt in them and many children and teenagers like the taste. Too much salt can lead to problems with high blood pressure and kidney problems in both children and teenagers, and as they become young adults, older teenagers must be careful not to get into the habit of eating more than 6g of salt a day.

Good, clear comparison of sugar intake and the potential problems associated with excess intake in both groups.

Good, clear comparison of salt intake and the potential problems associated with excess intake in both groups. The recommended maximum daily intake for children could also have been given.

Vitamin D and calcium are important nutrients for both groups. For children, their bones and second set of teeth are growing and they need calcium to be absorbed and laid down in their bones and teeth to make them strong and dense, so that when they are older, their bones reach peak bone mass and do not break very easily and their teeth do not decay easily. For teenagers, these nutrients are needed to produce new bone for the rapid growth spurts that take place during puberty and to maintain the strength of the bones once they have reached their full size and continue the process of reaching peak bone mass.

Good comparison of the needs for vitamin D and calcium, clearly showing differences in the two age groups as to why these nutrients are important.

Vitamin C is needed by both groups to absorb iron and make connective tissue and to carry oxygen round the body so they can get plenty of energy for all their activities. Iron will prevent anaemia, which can be common in teenage girls who lose blood during their periods. Some girls start their periods when they are still junior school age, so they also need enough iron. Anaemia makes people feel very tired and they find it difficult to concentrate at school. This is especially difficult for teenagers who have many exams to get through.

Good comparison for iron and vitamin C requirements, clearly showing the differences in requirement for both age groups.

Both groups need plenty of water to drink, to make sure they are properly hydrated. Dehydration is a common problem in children and teenagers, especially if they do not have easy access to water at school. It can put a strain on their kidneys and make them more likely to get urine infections. Children and teenagers should be encouraged to drink water, because they often choose sugary fizzy drinks rather than water, and this can lead to weight gain and tooth decay.

Clear comparison for water requirements between the two groups, highlighting similarities and differences. The same applies to dietary fibre.

Dietary fibre is important for both groups and they should eat plenty of wholegrain foods and fresh fruit and vegetables to make sure they have enough. In some children, constipation is a common problem and can lead to diseases of the intestines.

For the third part of Task 1 (AC1.3), you need to write about what happens to the body if people do not have the right amounts of nutrients (too much or not enough) – make sure you write about the target groups of people that are in the LAB.

Activity 22.2: Discuss the answers

Here are some example answers to help you see how much detail is needed in order to gain good marks. Compare the type and amount of detail that has been given for each answer.

With your class group, discuss why you think each answer has been awarded the level it has.

Example answers that would be awarded a Level 1 Pass (AC1.3)	Example answers that would be awarded a Level 2 Merit (AC1.3)
If people do not have enough protein they do not grow properly, their hair gets thin and they get weak nails. If they have too much protein, they may put on weight. Too much fat and carbohydrate can make people put on weight and get diseases such as heart attacks, obesity and Type 2 diabetes. Their liver may not work properly. If they do not have enough fat, they will lose weight and feel cold. If they do not have enough carbohydrate, they will not have enough energy. People can suffer if they do not have enough vitamins, e.g. children will not grow properly without enough vitamin A and they may go blind, and if they do not have enough vitamin D their bones will be weak and will bend because they have not got enough calcium in them. A lack of vitamin C will lead to scurvy and a lack of vitamin B1 will lead to beri-beri. If people do not have enough minerals, they can get diseases, e.g. not enough calcium will lead to weak bones, not enough iron will give them anaemia and not enough fluoride will make their teeth weak. People can also suffer if they have too much of some nutrients, e.g. too much sodium may give them high blood pressure, too much iron and vitamin A is poisonous, and too much fluoride can make their teeth go brown.	Children's and teenagers' bodies are growing and developing fast so they need a continuous supply of nutrients. When children do not have enough protein, they do not grow properly and are short for their age. Also, all their body processes that need a lot of protein, such as digesting food and absorbing nutrients, growing hair and having a healthy immune system to fight infections are all affected, which can make them very ill. Too much protein in the diet, which is quite common in countries such as the UK that eat a lot of meat and dairy foods, can put a strain on the kidneys and liver, which can be especially dangerous for younger children. If children and teenagers eat too many foods containing unrefined carbohydrate (especially free sugars) or fat, they are more likely to gain weight. These foods are energy dense and if the energy they contain is not all used up in physical exercise and activity, it may be stored as body fat. This can lead to other health problems such as obesity, heart disease and Type 2 diabetes. Obesity and Type 2 diabetes are becoming major health problems in children and teenagers in the UK and both have been linked to diet, weight gain and lack of activity. Both children and teenagers need to have enough dietary fibre in their diet to enable them to get rid of waste products from the body and prevent constipation and the possible development of other intestinal diseases such as bowel cancer and diverticular disease. Vitamin and mineral deficiencies are unusual to see in the UK, but some groups of children have developed rickets (where the bones become weak and bend under the weight of the body) due to a lack of vitamin D and calcium from the diet or limited exposure to sunlight. About 40% of peak bone mass is reached in adolescence, so it is essential for older children and teenagers to have enough calcium and vitamin D in their diet to let this happen. Older adults lose minerals from their bones as part of the natural aging process. If their bones are already weakened due to lack of vitamin D when they were younger, then their bones will lose minerals and become weak more quickly, which can lead to bone fractures and pain. Research shows that many children and teenagers do not eat enough fresh fruit and vegetables and probably do not have enough vitamin C in their diet. This can lead to scurvy, where red spots that you can see under the skin, mean that blood is leaking from blood vessels, because there is not enough vitamin C to make connective tissue to make the blood vessels strong. This will also mean that they do not absorb enough iron and are likely to develop anaemia as well. Teenage girls are more likely to develop anaemia because they lose blood during their periods. A deficiency of B vitamins is rare in the UK, but If children or teenagers follow a vegan diet, their parents need to make sure they get enough vitamin B12, as it is not easily found in plant foods and it is needed to make red blood cells and nerve cells in the brain and nervous system, which are developing fast. Both children and teenagers need to limit the amount of salt (sodium) they have in their diet. Children learn to like the taste of salt if they are regularly given foods such as crisps and other fried snacks, processed meats, takeaway foods and ready meals, many of which have a high salt content. Too much salt causes high blood pressure and puts a strain on the heart and kidneys. In children and teenagers, the kidneys are still developing, so this is dangerous.

For the fourth part of Task 1 (AC1.4), you need to write about how nutrients are affected when food is prepared and cooked. You could present the information as a chart, like the one below, but you must link it later to the dishes you choose to make to show how you would prevent too many nutrients being lost in your practical assessment:

Cooking method	Nutrient	Damaged by heat	Dissolves in water	Becomes easier to digest in the body	Notes
Boiling	Vitamins B_1, B_2, B_3, C	✓	✓		Use the cooking water in gravy, soup and sauces Up to 50% vitamin C is damaged when boiling green vegetables
	Calcium, sodium		✓		Use the cooking water in gravy, soup and sauces
	Starch			✓	Starch gelatinises
Steaming	Vitamin C	✓	✓		Only 15% is damaged
Poaching	Vitamins B_1, B_2, B_3	✓	✓		
Baking	Vitamins B_1, B_2, B_3, C	✓			
	Protein	✓			The high heat can overcook protein and make it hard to digest
Grilling	Vitamins B_1, B_2, B_3	✓			Up to 40% can be damaged by heat
Stir frying	Vitamin A			✓	The oil used can help the body absorb vitamin A from vegetables
	Vitamins B_1, B_2, B_3, C	✓	✓		Only a little damage as vegetables are cooked for a very short time
Roasting	Vitamins B_1, B_2, B_3, C	✓			High heat destroys most of the vitamin C and some of the B vitamins
All cooking methods	Protein			✓	Protein is denatured and coagulated, which makes it easier for the body to use. Too much high heat can overcook protein and make it hard to digest
	Fat	✓			If fat/oil is heated over and over again, it is gradually broken down into substances that harm the body

Stage 4
TASK 1: Write about menu planning for the target group in the LAB

In this stage of the LAB (LO2, AC2.1), you have to write about the factors to consider when choosing dishes for a menu. You need to link these to the LAB and in particular:

- The specific groups you are planning the menu for (in this example LAB it is children aged 5–12 years and teenagers aged 13–19 years).
- The venue (in this example LAB it is the cafe in a sports centre).
- The scenario (in this example you have to plan four dishes for the healthy and sustainable lunch menu that the management want to promote).

You can present your evidence as a table, as shown below, or a PowerPoint presentation:

Factors to consider in menu planning	Answers for the example LAB
Customers	Children aged 5–12 years: small portions for children need to be available. Menus should reflect current concerns over sugar and salt intake. Teenagers: menu items need to be affordable for teenagers with a limited amount of money to spend. Menus should include foods that provide a wide range of nutrients, in particular protein, calcium, vitamin C and iron. Menus should use a variety of cooking methods and limit the number of fried foods.
Price of the menu	There needs to be a range of prices available in the menu to suit the different amounts of money that children and teenagers can afford.
Finance, cost, customer budget	Menus may be priced so that children's meals are cheaper or part of a deal, e.g. children eat for free at certain times, in order to attract families with limited budgets. Special deals for teenage students may be offered on certain days or time of day.
Skills of the staff	The staff need to have the right skills to be able to produce the dishes in the menu. The three experienced chefs employed at the Ryeholt Sports Centre Cafe will be able to produce a varied menu. The open-plan kitchen in the cafe will enable them to be seen at work, which will attract customers.
Time of year, seasonality, season of event	Ryeholt Sports Centre will need to order ingredients from a variety of sources, and may be able to buy seasonal ingredients from farms and producers in the local area. The menu can be changed to suit the season and seasonal sports.
Equipment available	The menu will need to be matched to the equipment in the kitchen, e.g. if the chefs want to make fruit smoothies in the summer, there needs to be enough storage space for the fruit they use and the right equipment to make them.
Time available	The cafe will cater for the various needs of the visitors to the sports centre, so will need to be able to provide meals/snacks throughout the day, as well as the evening. This will require careful planning so that there are enough chefs on duty throughout the day and evening to produce the meals in time, and enough storage facilities to allow ingredients to be prepared in advance and stored safely.

Type of provision	The menu provided by Ryeholt Sports Centre Cafe needs to be varied and diverse to cater for the likely range of customers. It will be a good idea to have several planned that are rotated, e.g. every week, in order to offer variations on a regular basis.
	The promotion of environmental sustainability needs to be very visible to get customers on board with the idea, e.g. placing recycling information and bins in a prominent place (such as a recycling hub in reception), including information on posters, information sheets and screens, etc.
	The menus need to be planned carefully to make sure that enough, but not too many, ingredients are in stock in order to avoid food and money wastage.

You then have to explain how the dishes for the cafe menu will deal with environmental issues (AC2.2).

As you can only achieve a maximum of a Level 2 Pass for this part of the assessment, you could present your work in the form of a chart or a mini poster that could be put into the menu folder in the cafe, on the reception desk and on screens throughout the building to tell customers about how the sports centre addresses environmental issues, like this example:

Ryeholt Sports Club

 ## and the environment

At Ryeholt Sports Club, we have pledged to minimise our impact on the environment. This is how we are doing it:

 When we plan our menus for the cafe, we carefully consider where the food we buy comes from. We buy as many ingredients as we can from local producers, so that we can use seasonal foods and reduce food miles and pollution from transport and delivery vehicle emissions. We use misshapen vegetables and fruits to prevent them from being wasted.

 We have made the decision to reduce our use of plastics because of current and ongoing concerns over land and sea pollution, e.g. we use only metal cutlery and china plates and dishes in the cafe and have replaced plastic drinking straws with paper ones.

 We only buy ingredients and materials from suppliers who use very little or no plastic packaging.

 We recycle plastic packaging and other items, e.g. bottles, cardboard boxes, etc., and we use takeaway containers made from materials that can be recycled, e.g. aluminium foil, card.

 We do not use individually wrapped items such as seasonings, butter, sauces, jams and we use ingredients such as spices, flavourings, sauces, etc., that come in refillable or recyclable catering-sized containers.

 We buy cleaning liquids in large containers and pour them into reusable smaller bottles.

 In our customer toilets, we have replaced paper towels with solar-powered electric hand-driers.

 We encourage our customers to refill their own drinking bottles from our water fountains, rather than buying bottled water. We do the same with takeaway coffee and tea by selling re-usable takeaway cups in reception.

Stage 5
Write about your ideas for some dishes that would be suitable for the target group in the LAB

In this stage of the LAB (AC2.3), you need to start thinking about which dishes you are going to choose and plan to make for the practical assessment (Stage 9, Task 3). There is no set rule about when you should start to do this, but now would be a suitable time, as it will help you to answer AC2.3.

You need to carry out some research for recipes that would be suitable lunch dishes for the two specified groups in the LAB. Remember that your task is to suggest **four** dishes for the lunch menu that would appeal to primary schoolchildren and teenagers. At least two dishes should be main courses; the other two can be starters or desserts or one of each. The dishes should demonstrate at least three food preparation skills and three cooking methods.

Stage 6
Choose dishes you will make for the target group in the LAB in your practical assessment

From the four dishes you have researched and chosen, choose **two** of them to make for your practical assessment. Make sure the two dishes show at least three food preparation skills and three cooking methods between them (a reminder of these is shown below):

Food preparation skills and techniques	Cooking methods
Blending	Baking
Bread making	Blanching
Chopping/knife skills	Boiling
Creativity	Braising
Dough making, e.g. pastries, biscuits	Chilling
Garnishing	Cooling
Hydrating	Frying: deep/shallow pan frying, stir frying, dry frying
Kneading	Grilling (griddling)
Melting	Hot holding
Peeling	Poaching
Portion control	Roasting
Positioning on serving dish	Sautéing
Rubbing-in	Steaming
Segmenting	Stewing
Setting with gelatine	
Shaping	
Sieving	
Slicing	
Weighing and measuring	
Whisking	

Here are the four chosen dishes for the example LAB and the food preparation skills and cooking methods they use:

Chosen dishes	Food preparation skills and techniques used	Cooking methods use
Mini vegetable pasties (made with wholemeal flour), with mixed salad	*Vegetable preparation* • Peeling, chopping *Pastry making* • Rubbing-in, shaping, crimping, glazing • Garnishing	Sautéing Boiling Baking

Chicken curry made with coconut milk and served with wholegrain rice	*Chicken preparation* • Skinning, de-boning, cutting chicken thighs *Vegetable preparation* • Peeling, chopping, dicing • Garnishing	Boiling Sautéing Stewing
Lentil burgers in wholemeal rolls, vegan coleslaw and roasted root wedges	*Vegetable preparation* • Peeling, chopping, slicing, dicing • Garnishing • Bread making • Kneading • Shaping • Blending ingredients for vegan mayonnaise	Boiling Pan frying Baking Roasting
Panna cotta and fresh fruit	• Setting a mixture with gelatine • Decorating with fruit • Fruit preparation	Heating milk and cream

Once you have chosen your dishes, you will have completed Task 1.

Stage 7

TASK 2: Write about the factors you have considered when planning your chosen dishes for the target group in the LAB

Explain clearly and in detail the factors you have considered when choosing your four dishes and how they meet the needs of children and teenagers (AC2.4). Use your class notes to help.

You could set out the information about your chosen dishes as shown in a chart like this:

Chosen dish	Nutrition	Cost	Organoleptic (sensory appeal)
Chicken curry with wholegrain rice	The chicken and rice provide protein. The curry spices and wholegrain rice provide a good source of iron. The rice and vegetables in the curry provide carbohydrate for energy, as well as dietary fibre. The coconut milk provides fat for energy. The dish provides a range of vitamins.	Chicken is a relatively low-cost meat, and the rice and vegetables are also relatively low cost. This means that the cost of the dish would be affordable for the target groups.	**Flavour / taste:** the dish provides a range of flavours from the spices, coconut milk and vegetables. **Texture:** the sauce is smooth, and the chicken and vegetables are tender. The rice adds texture to the dish. **Aroma:** the aroma of the curry spices adds to the appeal of the dish. **Appearance:** the curry sauce is a good contrast to the rice. Vegetables such as sweetcorn and peas could be added to the rice for additional colour, flavour, texture and nutrients.

Vegetable pasties and salad 	Suitable for lacto-vegetarians. The meal provides a wide range of nutrients required by children and teenagers, especially calcium and vitamin D, some iron, fibre, vitamin C and vitamins A, E and B group. The vegetables (which include beans) and the flour both provide plant protein. The vegetables provide carbohydrate for energy, as well as dietary fibre, vitamins and minerals. The fat in the pastry also provides energy. Cheese (if used), is a useful source of protein, calcium and other minerals and vitamins.	Vegetables that are in season can be used. The overall cost of producing the pasties would be cheaper than making meat pasties.	**Flavour/taste:** the dish provides a range of flavours from the different well-seasoned vegetables used and the cheese (if used). **Texture:** there are a variety of textures e.g. crispy, short pastry, tender vegetables in pasties, crisp lettuce and other salad ingredients. The salad adds texture to the whole dish. **Aroma:** the aroma of the vegetables and baked cheese adds to the appeal of the dish. **Appearance:** the pasties are a traditional shape. The range of colours (e.g. bright colours of lettuce contrast with golden pastry) is appealing to customers. Vegetables in the salad give additional colour, flavour, texture and nutrients.
Lentil burgers in wholemeal rolls, vegan coleslaw and roasted beetroot, sweet potato and butternut squash wedges 	Suitable for vegans. Lentils and nuts in the burgers, wheat in the bread rolls and tofu and cashew nuts in the vegan mayonnaise all provide plant protein as well as other nutrients such as carbohydrate, iron, calcium and B vitamins. The raw vegetables in the coleslaw and the roasted beetroot and sweet potato and butternut squash wedges provide a variety of vitamins including vitamin A (beta carotene) and vitamin C.	Lentils and other vegetables are a low-cost source of protein. Root vegetables are relatively inexpensive.	A variety of crisp roasted root vegetables and coleslaw give a variety of colours, flavours and textures. The wholemeal rolls should have a soft texture inside and crust on the outside.
Panna cotta and fresh fruit 	The dish provides a range of nutrients needed by this age group, especially protein, calcium and vitamin D. The fresh fruit provides fibre, antioxidants and vitamin C.	The fresh fruit can be varied according to the season and cost.	The sharpness of the fresh fruit combines well with the smooth, sweet panna cotta. The fresh fruits provide colour, texture and flavour.

All of the chosen dishes would be suitable for children and teenagers, but in order to allow for the differences in the amount of food that each group needs, their appetite and how much they could manage to eat, each dish could be available in two portion sizes (small and large). This would prevent wastage and would also mean a price difference (the smaller portion would be cheaper than the larger portion). This may also be preferred by those children and teenagers who want to spend less money on their lunch, so will choose a smaller portion.

Stage 8
TASK 2: Write a production plan for your chosen dishes

You must produce an **annotated** and **dovetailed timed production plan** (AC2.4) for the **two** chosen dishes you will make in the practical assessment, which should all be cooked within the same time frame.

An example is given below for the two chosen dishes from the example LAB. The plan has been colour-coded to show which dish is being made, and annotated to show the special points you need to remember when making the dishes.

For maximum marks, the annotated production plan must include all of the following:

- Quantities of different ingredients needed
- Equipment needed
- Mise en place (getting ready and organised before you start preparing and cooking the food)
- Timing – for preparing, cooking, decorating, etc.
- Sequencing – the order in which you prepare and cook the food (including dovetailing)
- Cooling food down – where, how and for how long you will do this, and at what temperature
- Hot holding – how you will keep food hot and at what temperature
- Completion – how you will know your dish is finished
- Serving/presentation
- Removal of waste
- Contingencies – e.g. what will you have ready in case something goes wrong
- Health, safety and hygiene points
- Quality points
- Storage of the food during the practical assessment so that it stays safe to eat.

Production plan for:

Chicken curry made with coconut milk and served with wholegrain rice

Lentil burgers in wholemeal rolls, vegan coleslaw, roasted root wedges

Time: 09.15 – 12.00

Key: **C** = Contingency   **HSH** =Health, Safety and Hygiene point   **QP** = Quality point

---

Quantities of ingredients needed

Chicken curry made with coconut milk and served with wholegrain rice (makes 4 large or 8 small portions):

8 chicken thighs, 2 tbsp oil, 1 large onion (finely diced), 1 large courgette (finely diced), 1 large red pepper (finely diced), 1 medium carrot (finely diced), a piece of fresh ginger – approx. 5cm – peeled and finely chopped, 3 tsp ground coriander, 2 tbsp fennel seeds, 3 tsp ground cumin, 2 tsp ground turmeric, 1 medium can coconut milk, I small carton coconut cream, 2 tbsp onion, rhubarb or apple chutney, 4 tbsp chopped fresh coriander, 200ml water; 60g uncooked brown rice **per serving**

Lentil burgers in wholemeal rolls, vegan coleslaw, and roasted root wedges (makes 4 large or 8 small portions):

Rolls: 225g Strong plain wholemeal flour, ¼ level teaspoon salt, 160 ml warm water, ½ tsp dried, fast-acting yeast ; **Burgers:** (this recipe uses cup measurements) 1 cup cooked brown rice, 1¾ cups cooked brown lentils, 1 medium onion (peeled and chopped into 4 pieces), 2 cloves garlic, peeled, 1 cup diced sweet potato (raw), ½ cup walnuts or pecans, ⅓ cup tomato or brown ketchup, 1 tbsp Dijon mustard, 3 tbsp ground linseeds, ½ tsp salt, ¼ tsp cayenne pepper, freshly ground black pepper, ¾ cup fine cornmeal (yellow polenta); **Vegan mayonnaise and coleslaw:** 150g firm silken tofu, ¼ cup raw cashew nuts (unsalted), 2 tbsp lemon juice, 1 tsp rice vinegar, 2 tbsp cider vinegar, 1 tsp runny honey, ¼ tsp salt, ½ tsp Dijon mustard; ¼ small white cabbage, 4 spring onions, 1 carrot, 1 small red eating apple, 2 sticks celery; **Roasted vegetables:** 1 medium red onion, 2 medium carrots, 1 medium parsnip, 2 medium potatoes, 1 medium raw beetroot, 4 tbsp olive oil, seasoning; **To finish burgers:** salad garnish (lettuce, tomato, cucumber)

Equipment needed

Chicken curry made with coconut milk and served with wholegrain rice:

Meat knife, red chopping board, vegetable knife, green chopping board, large saucepan with lid, medium saucepan, colander

Lentil burgers in wholemeal rolls, vegan coleslaw, and roasted root wedges:

Two mixing bowls, wooden spoon, three baking trays, electric food processor, electric blender, vegetable knife, green chopping board, brown chopping board, mixing bowl, shallow roasting tin, non-stick baking paper

Time	Activity	Notes (annotations)
09.15	Mise en place: line baking trays, weigh/measure ingredients, place cashew nuts in a bowl covered with cold water (for mayonnaise) and leave to soak; organise all ingredients.	**HSH** Place chicken thighs and coconut cream in refrigerator until used.
09.30	Bread rolls: make dough for bread rolls, cover and leave to rise in a warm place until doubled in size. Lentil burgers: Place rice and lentils into separate saucepans with water and bring to the boil. Simmer until soft – approximately 15–20 minutes for each.	**C** If dough is slow to rise, place mixing bowl containing dough into a larger bowl of warm water and cover with a clean cloth.
09.55	Clear away and wash up. Throw away any rubbish and waste.	**HSH** Wash hands thoroughly after handling rubbish.
10.05	Drain rice and lentils, cover and set aside.	
10.10	Chicken curry: remove the skin and bones from the chicken thighs and chop the chicken into bite-size pieces. Coat the chicken pieces with dried the spices by stirring them well in a mixing bowl.	**HSH** Use red chopping board. Do not wash the raw chicken. Wash and dry hands thoroughly after handling raw chicken.
10.30	Clear away and wash up. Throw away any rubbish and waste.	**HSH** Wash hands thoroughly after handling rubbish. Make sure all raw chicken pieces are washed off board and knife.
10.35	Chicken curry: chop all the vegetables for the curry, and peel and grate the ginger. In large saucepan, sauté the vegetables in the oil for 5 minutes with the lid on. Add chicken pieces and sauté for another 10 minutes, stirring occasionally.	**HSH** Use green chopping board.
10.38	While chicken is being sautéed, clear away and wash up. Throw away any rubbish and waste.	**HSH** Wash hands thoroughly after handling rubbish.
10.43	Lentil burgers: place onion, garlic, sweet potato and nuts into food processor. Process for a few seconds until all finely chopped. Add the cooked rice and cooked lentils and process for a few seconds. Place mixture in a large mixing bowl. Add mustard, ketchup, linseed, cayenne pepper, salt and a few twists of freshly ground black pepper. Mix together thoroughly. Add the cornmeal and mix in well. Divide the mixture into four and shape into large burgers. Place burgers on non-stick paper on a baking tray. Place in refrigerator until ready to bake.	Switch on the oven to gas 7 / 220°C (200°C electric fan oven) **C** Have a little extra cornmeal available to add to the mixture if it is a bit wet.

10.45	Chicken curry: add the coconut milk, coconut cream, grated ginger, chutney and water. Stir well, and simmer for a further 20 minutes, stirring occasionally.	**QP** Stir frequently to prevent the curry from sticking to the base of the pan and burning, which would spoil the flavour.
10.50	Bread rolls: check bread dough, knead and divide into 4 rolls. Shape into baps (flattened rolls). Place on greased baking tray and allow to rise for 15 minutes.	**QP** The rolls will increase in size when they are baked. Allow for this when trying to make sure that the burgers and rolls will be the same size when cooked.
10.55	Roasted vegetables: chop vegetables for roasting and mix with oil and seasoning in a large mixing bowl. Place in a roasting tin. Place in oven for 25–40 minutes, until tender and crisp.	**QP** Leave skins on (apart from onion) for extra texture. Stir vegetables occasionally during the roasting time.
11.00	Clear away and wash up. Throw away any rubbish and waste.	**HSH** Wash hands thoroughly after handling rubbish.
11.05	Bread rolls: place bread rolls in oven and bake for 12–15 minutes until well risen and crusty.	
11.06	Chicken curry: check chicken is cooked in curry and turn off the heat. Stir in 3 tbsp of chopped coriander. Save 1 tbsp for garnish. Place in serving dish, cover and keep hot. Heat water for cooking the brown rice.	**HSH** The curry must be kept hot at a minimum core temperature of 63°C.
11.10	Place rice in boiling water and simmer for 15 minutes or until tender. Lentil burgers: place burgers in oven for 15 minutes – turn them over and bake for another 15 minutes.	**C** Have some boiling water available in case rice needs more water.
11.20	Check rolls and remove if baked. Place on a cooling tray	**QP** The baps should sound hollow when tapped with the fingers.
11.25	Clear away and wash up. Throw away any rubbish and waste. Turn burgers over and replace in oven for a further 15 minutes. Check rice and drain water if cooked. Keep rice hot in a covered serving dish.	**HSH** Wash hands thoroughly after handling rubbish.
11.30	Vegan mayonnaise: drain water from the cashew nuts and place these and all other ingredients into electric blender. Blend until smooth. Check roasted vegetables and if tender, keep hot in oven.	**C** Add a little water if the mixture is too thick.
11.35	Coleslaw: slice the ingredients for the coleslaw and mix with the mayonnaise. Place in serving dish and chill in refrigerator.	
11.40	Remove burgers from oven and keep them warm.	**QP** Cover with foil to prevent them from drying out.
11.50	Lentil burgers: assemble lentil burgers and place inside baps with salad garnish. Serve each burger with a portion of roasted vegetables and a portion of coleslaw.	**QP** Serve on warm plates, apart from coleslaw, which should be served in a small cold dish or ramekin (to keep it cold) then placed on the main plate.
11.55	Serve curry with rice and garnish with coriander.	**QP** Serve on a warm plate.
12.00	Final clear away and wash up. Throw away any rubbish and waste.	**HSH** Wash hands thoroughly after handling rubbish.

Once you have written your production plan, you will have completed Task 2.

Stage 9
TASK 3: Prepare, cook and present your dishes for the target group in the LAB and take photographs of the results

Task 3 is your chance to showcase your practical and creative skills by making the dishes you have chosen and written a production plan for. In order to achieve your best result, you need to be able to show that you can do all of the following:

- Use a range of **food preparation techniques** and **cooking methods** with **ability** and **skill (competence)**, **confidence**, **care** and **accuracy (precision)** and **speed**.
- Work independently.
- Show good **food safety** and **hygiene** practices during **preparation, food storage, cooking, serving, washing up** and **waste disposal**.
- Check the **quality** of the **commodities** you use throughout their **preparation, cooking** and **serving**.
- Produce dishes that have a **high quality** for **flavour, texture, aroma, creativity** and **appearance**.

Completed dishes:

Chicken curry made with coconut milk and served with wholegrain rice

Lentil burgers in wholemeal rolls, vegan coleslaw, and roasted root wedges

Picture credits

Alamy Stock Photo

p17 Patti McConville; p54 Science Photo Library; p55 PHOVOIR; p61 dpa picture alliance archive; p61 Wavebreakmedia Ltd UC77; p86 Ernie Janes; p91 Art Directors & TRIP; p117 Kay Roxby; p117 Dorling Kindersley ltd; p117 OneDayOneImage; p117 pixel shepherd; p117 Simply Signs; p133 James Jackson; p133 Zoonar GmbH; p138 Pamela Maxwell; p138 Art Directors & TRIP; p138 blickwinkel; p155 Jeffrey Isaac Greenberg 7; p157 Yuliya Furman; p158 MBI; p166 funkyfood London - Paul Williams.

Shutterstock.com

p4 elenabsl; p6 Emma Adams Photography, THE SinCos Studio, fotosunny, Ceri Breeze, Laboo Studio, Cedric Weber, Africa Studio, David Tadevosian, CandyBox Images; p7 Maridav, In-Finity, Vassamon Anansukkasem, galaira, ngaga; p8 In-Finity, galaira, ngaga; p9 In-Finity; p12 navorolphotography; p15 Alemon cz; p16 jesterpop, stockfour, Gorodenkoff, Syda Productions; p17 wavebreakmedia, SpeedKingz, Roman Kosolapov; p18 nutcd32; p20 dokurose, icedea, Lisovskaya Natalia, ShaunWilkinson, ideyweb, amophoto_au, FabrikaSimf; p21 Anna Malygina, Andrey_Popov, Josep Suria, Hunter Bliss Images, from my point of view; p22 vectorfusionart, wavebreakmedia, Georgejmclittle; p23 MK photograp55, Chesky, graphego, Proxima Studio; p24 Matylda Laurence, phBodrova, James Mattil, kongsky, sirtravelalot; p25 Trendsetter Images, Syda Productions, ESB basic, Alena Ozerova, Aila Images; p26 bsd, Barry Barnes, RedlineVector, creativepriyanka, danjazzia; p27 ober-art, TunedIn by Westend61, Jacob Blount, wavebreakmedia, mnimage, images72; p30 ArnaPhoto, Sabuhi Novruzov, T VECTOR ICONS, Norenko Andrey, Benn Beckman, veronchick_84, BimXD, Altagracia Art, Vladvm , Sulee_R, Wor Sang Jun, Janis Abolins; p31 bonchan, Vitezslav Valka, Satika, ProstoSvet, Taras Vyshnya; p32 Sergey Ryzhov; p33 Pavel Kubarkov, vectorfusionart, Oleksandr_Delyk, anmbph, Alena Brozova; p34 SimpleVector [NECJ=KTIE], Syda Productions, Kasa_s; p35 Leremy, LightField Studios , Leremy, the Proicon, Inotlus, RedKoala, Arcady, Leremy, Aha-Soft, Leremy; p37 a2l, zhu difeng, wavebreakmedia; p38 fiphoto, Petar Djordjevic; p39 Sergey Spritnyuk, TravnikovStudio, Monkey Business Images, SONTAYA CHAISAMUTR, UfaBizPhoto, Iakov Filimonov; p40 Technicsorn Stocker, pariwat pannium, Andrey_Popov, ReneGamper, Sheila Fitzgerald, anmbph, exopixel; p41 LightField Studios, David Tadevosian, Fototocam, Pranch, Alexis C, Lemberg Vector studio, testing; p42 MemoryMan; p43 William Perugini, Yulia Davidovich, Sukpaiboonwat, paseven; p44 NavinTar, Arina P Habich, AS photo studio, Vectomart, Rawpixel.com, Sveta Evglevskaia; p45 Atstock Productions, Ministr-84, David MG; p47 Monkey Business Images, Paul Daniels; p50 Rainer Lesniewski, Lemurik; p51 Peter Etchells, Peter Etchells, Tyler Olson, -Taurus-, Peter Etchells, Andrey_Popov, Budimir Jevtic; p52 a_v_d, Rainer Lesniewski, Ariene Studio, Venot, Albo003; p54 Alta Oosthuizen, pimchawee, Beetroot Studio; p55 v74, Vera Larina, THANISORN PANYA; p56 Yu_Zhdanova, Phovoir; p57 Have a nice day Photo, wavebreakmedia, Phovoir, oneSHUTTER oneMEMORY, fossil_k, Neo Studio, MIA Studio; p58 JL-Pfeifer, Gorodenkoff; p59 adriaticfoto, wavebreakmedia, Wittybear, ambrozinio; p60 Andrey_Popov, Inked Pixels, Peter Gudella , mikumistoc, photographyfirm , Richard Peterson, Richard z , Sasin Paraksa; p61 Africa Studio, wavebreakmedia, Sopotnicki, KenKitti, SteveWoods, Claudio Divizia; p62 CoolVectorStock , olegganko, graficriver_icons_logo, phipatbig, Panptys, Martial Red, Powerful Design, AVIcon, Martial Red, Richard z , Kilroy79; p65 Leremy; p66 Gang Liu, showcake, Mikhail Valeev , Leremy, gresei , Phovoir, DisobeyArt , SHUKASAMI, Blue Pig , Bahadir Yeniceri, marcin jucha, David Fedulov, JIANG HONGYAN, Claudio Divizia, Oleg Golovnev, Jiri Hera, margouillat photo, mimagephotography, Aaron Amat; p67 Mikhail Valeev , Africa Studio, gresei , Phovoir, Bahadir Yeniceri, Gayvoronskaya_Yana, Timolina, David Fedulov, JIANG HONGYAN, Oleg Golovnev, margouillat photo, Olga Nayashkova, Vicki Vale, Aaron Amat, Markus Mainka; p68 Maks Narodenko, M. Unal Ozmen, Joe Gough, justsolove, Jiri Hera, Lano Lan, Mongolka, Anton Starikov, ULKASTUDIO, Elena Elisseeva, ducu59us; p69 Sven Hastedt, koosen, Gertjan Hooijer, Dmitriy Krasko; p70 Vlad Siaber, KOOKLE, photogal; p71 Alis Leonte, chaphot, Amy Kerkemeyer; p72 Africa Studio, kaband, Hong Vo, vitals, Africa Studio, MaraZe, Moving Moment, Billion-Photos2, Kaiskynet Studio, 1989studio, Pakhnyushchy, Kateryna Bibro, Maks Narodenko; p73 photocritical, Marochkina Anastasiia, Africa Studio; p74 Dolvalol; p76 SnvvSnvvSnvv, grafvision, s_oleg, grafvision, BasPhoto, photogal, JaffarAliAfzal123, travelpeter, 279photo Studio, Peter Turner Photography, Baloncici, andyparker72, 1000 Words, Max Maier, Africa Studio, vectorfusionart, Ron Ellis, Tupungato, Ideya,

Terence Mendoza; p80 Anton Veselov; p81 hxdbzxy, Dani Vincek, April909, Narattapon Purod, JIANG HONGYAN, Leremy, studio on line, Fotovika; p82 Monkey Business Images, Steve Cukrov, Romariolen, pathdoc, Fotovika; p83 Stephm2506; p85 lensmen, wavebreakmedia; p86 Ruslan Huzau, Pegasene, Cegli, navee sangvitoon, Tomasz Klejdysz; p89 ARTYOORAN; p91 Nina Rubanyuk, Ilya Andriyanov; p92 Leremy, Leremy, Leremy, Monkey Business Images; p93 Leremy, Leremy, Leremy, Yayayoyo, Leremy, Yayayoyo, Yayayoyo, Leremy; p99 jorrisg, ThanasStudio, andrzej80, icede; p102 Syda Productions; p105 bitt24, DisobeyArt, Africa Studio, Christos Georghiou, Diana Taliun, In Green, joshya, ksenvitaln, La Gorda, Maxx-Studio, Nattika, Rka Koka, tamsindove, vovan; p106 oknoart, Silberkorn, Lightspring, Alila Medical Media, Tom Wang, corbac40, Ekaterina Markelova, bikeriderlondon, bikeriderlondon, Christos Georghiou, CLIPAREA l Custom media, Diana Taliun, Evan Lorne, George Dolkijh, holbox, joshya, Production Perig, Stokkete, studiovin; p108 Yanas, Karen Struthers, Mega Pixel, Billion Photos, Konstantin Kopachinsky, puhhha, K2 PhotoStudio, Alexander Raths; p111 Sea Wave, ht- margouillat photo, sasimoto, Lightspring, leonori, Lisovskaya Natalia, Shawn Hempel, symbiot, baibaz, eZeePics, Alexander Raths, Anna Sedneva, Coprid, leonori, marco mayer; p112 Serhiy Shullye, M. Unal Ozmen, ignatius 63, Coffeemill, Moving Moment, Moving Moment, leonori, Kostin, TorriPhoto, Bahadir Yeniceri, ConstantinosZ, Alexander Raths, Nata-Lia, Somchai Som, MAHATHIR MOHD YASIN, Shining stars, Veselka, xamnesiacx, Abramova Elena, SMDSS, Kerdkanno, iprachenko, monticello, Dionisvera, liza54500, Yaroslav Mishin, Africa Studio, RTimages, marco mayer; p113 Sea Wave, AlinaMD, S-F, Robyn Mackenzie, aboikis, Morinka, Hong Vo, Billion Photos, Danny Smythe, iprachenko, liza54500, Africa Studio, ooddysmile stocker, chrisdorney, Rugged Studio, Robyn Mackenzie, Joe Gough; p114 multiart, Leremy, Leremy, Zern Liew, Blue Planet Earth, Volodymyr Krasyuk, Leremy, Bro Studio, Wision, Syda Productions; p115 gorillaimages, meaofoto, allstars, chrisdorney, Edward Westmacott, Kay_MoTec, Mikhail Valeev, Moving Moment, rukxstockphoto, Yu_Zh; p118 VGstockstudio, kyozstorage_stock, Evgeny Litvinov, NatashaPhoto; p119 Leremy, vectorchef, Leremy, Leremy; p120 Mihai Simonia, Sunny Forest, Eric Gevaert, OMMB, Dmytro Gilitukha, BABYFRUITY, MOHAMED ABDULRAHEEM, Marian Weyo, Pixel 4 Images, Dirk Ercken, aleksandr hunta; p121 Enriscapes, BlueOrange Studio, Paparacy, larry mcguirk, zaemiel, Sibuet Benjamin, Kzenon; p122 Moving Moment, Ryco Montefont, Valeria Aksakova, EQRoy, natashamam, Lonspera, Salvomassara, irabel8, Anatolii Riepin; p123 Catarina Vaz; p124 Richard Pinder, Teguh Mujiono.tif, Jovanovic Dejan, Irina Bg, Brian A Jackson, holbox, Jovanovic Dejan; p125 schankz, Yayayoyo, Milles Studio, White78, Jovanovic Dejan, Andrey_Popov, Yayayoyo; p126 Andrei Iakhniuk, martiapunts.tif, Paul_Brighton, Teguh Mujiono, pavla, Jovanovic Dejan, Karolina Awizen; p127 Vintagepix, Olha Solodenko, rainbow33, amenic181, Audi Dela Cruz, October22, Joe Gough; p128 VectorPlotnikoff, YourElechka, Arina P Habich, Monkey Business Images, siridhata, Marchie, Abscent, udra11, wideonet, baibaz, Lia Li; p134 ND700, Alexander Raths; p135 Martina V, baibaz; p136 allstars, photobeps; p137 IZZ HAZEL, naito29, Elizabeth A.Cummings, Viktor1; p138 Lydia Vero, Gumpanat, Amawasri Pakdara, M. Unal Ozmen, AN NGUYEN, David Smart, gowithstock, Igor Dutina, Brilliance stock, Edward Westmacott, bigacis, Syda Productions, Anton Starikov, monticello, Nattika; p139 Viktorija Reuta, Africa Studio, Cattlaya Art; p140 zi3000, Ugorenkov Aleksandr, Feng Yu, BalancePhoto, studiovin, Jiri Hera, Ruslans Golenkovs, Radu Bercan, Piyato, Ilya Andriyanov, doomu, Africa Studio; p141 New Africa, galitsin, stockfour, siloto, Ina Ts, Africa Studio, Nomad_Soul, Elena Elisseeva, 135pixels, ersin ergin, Syda Productions, Alina Kholopova, Studio 72, 4_mai; p142 A'photophy; p143 hlphoto; p144 kazoka, Robyn Mackenzie, KorolDenis; p145 koss13; p146 Marian Fil, Africa Studio, Lukas Gojda; p147 Dan70, Branislav Nenin, SeDmi; p148 L Mirror, Andrey_Popov, InnerVisionPRO; p149 Evgeny Pyatkov, Andrew Humphries, Kokliang; p150 Viacheslav Nikolaenko, Lyudvig Aristarhovich, Smit; p151 Vanillasky Friday, keko64, JM Travel Photography, bonchan, FoodAndPhoto, PYP, MaraZe, Sylvia sooyoN, Flipser, alex_gor, Prostock-studio; p152 lex Tihonovs, Brent Hofacker, Jacek Chabraszewski, Ryzhkov Photography, Paulo Vilela, Daria Proskuryakova, jabiru, stoica ionela, 694457572Maria Medvedeva; p153 timages, Monkey Business Images, Lesya Dolyuk, Gavran333; p155 seyomedo; p157 Lena Serditova, Tatiana Bralnina, NIKI90, Eladora, bitt24; p162 ESB Professional, Tim Large, Kraphix, Maxx-Studio, Waraporn Chokchaiworarat, Lena Pan, Jacob Lund; p163 ubonwanu, Yuliyan Velchev, graphego, Rashevskyi Viacheslav, JUN3; p165 Anton Merzlyakov, Ingridsl; p166 mpessaris, sarsmis; p169 Anton Merzlyakov; p170 michaeljung, Dmitry Kalinovskiy, Rommel Canlas, Sergey Chumakov